SAP

Coaching
Winning Basketball with
the Overplay-Pressure
Defense

Coaching
Winning Basketball with
the Overplay-Pressure
Defense

Ken Johnson

Parker Publishing Company, Inc.
West Nyack, New York

Library of Congress Cataloging in Publication Data

Johnson, Ken.
  Coaching winning basketball with the overplay-
pressure defense.

  Includes index.
  1. Basketball—Defense. 2. Basketball coaching.
I. Title.
GV888.J63   796.32'32   81-14017
ISBN 0-13-139121-6 AACR2

Dedication:

This book is dedicated to my wife, Vicki, and to my son, Chad.

Foreword

There is a very good reason why Ken Johnson became successful coaching and writing about overplay-pressure, man-to-man defenses. That style of basketball requires intensity, desire and dedication—all attributes Johnson possesses in great abundance.

Once I wrote that he "eats, sleeps and lives basketball" because that's exactly what Ken Johnson is all about. The University of Wisconsin assistant coach comes from a family of basketball coaches that includes his father, Mel, a hall of fame high school coach in Illinois, as well as brothers Ron and Roger.

Ken once told me, "I love the game of basketball and I think I could be happy coaching sixth grade basketball in the elementary school or almost anywhere. I love it that much."

When he attended UW-La Crosse, the Indians were not expected to produce much basketball excitement, but it was Ken's brand of fervor and dedication that enabled them to play in two National Association of Intercollegiate Athletics (NAIA) tournaments during his four years there.

His coaching records at Hinsdale and Elgin, Ill., attest to the quality of his teaching technique. Wisconsin struggled during Ken's first season as Bill Cofield's assistant, but the Badgers did shock Illinois at Champaign, upset Ohio State, and knock Minnesota out of an NCAA bid by displaying the same kind of defensive intensity espoused by Johnson.

Johnson also carried a heavy load of Cofield's recruiting during his first year on the staff, and neutral observers contend Wisconsin landed one of the best freshman classes in the Big Ten. UW Athletic Director Elroy "Crazylegs" Hirsch credited Johnson with much of the recruiting success and said, "Ken did just a fantastic job." Johnson's coaching honesty, sincerity and tenacity paid off again, this time as a recruiter.

By Tom Butler
State Journal sports reporter

What This Book Will Do for You

Coaching Winning Basketball with the Overplay-Pressure Defense is a step-by-step plan for developing a consistently winning program. It is a defensive system that can totally dominate any offense and can be effective regardless of the type of personnel you may have. No longer do you have to hide your team's defensive weaknesses in a sloppy makeshift defense and watch your opponents scorch the nets with easy jump shots. This is a defense that can attack the offense and completely disrupt their game plan.

I have used this defensive system at two high schools that had had strong losing traditions in basketball. The overplay-pressure man-to-man defense completely turned both schools' teams into winners. Time and time again this system has controlled the tempo of the game.

What do you think your chances of winning would be if you had control of the opponent's offense? If you could dictate when and where the offensive team's shots would be taken, the pendulum of victory would swing strongly in your favor. The overplay-pressure man-to-man defense can do these things and more. It breaks up the timing of the opponents' offensive plays, hurries their shots, forces errant passes and makes ball-handling extremely difficult.

The general principles governing the overplay-pressure man-to-man defense are specially developed in this book to counter any type of offensive strategy. The passing game, the screen and roll, the shuffle movement, the slow down, the fast break, and the stall offenses can all be handled with this defensive philosophy. The overplay-pressure man-to-man can stop them all.

Rebounding superiority on the defensive end of the court is another important quality of this intense style of play. The opposition is usually forced so far from the basket that defensive rebounding superiority is assured. Because of the unusual amount of defensive pressure applied, a larger offensive team's size advantage may be neutralized and actually become a liability.

Now, add the half-court overplay-pressure man-to-man to the full-court overplay-pressure gang presses, and your opponents are in trouble. They may feel that your team is using six men rather than five in the game. There will be a sixth man on the court all right—it'll be the overplay-pressure defensive system at work. Once the defenses begin to mesh, your opponents will be in total confusion trying to figure out exactly what type of defense is being played.

The first time we used this defense, the opponent's coach asked us to please tell him what type of defense we had played. It can be absolutely devastating at times. We stopped one team from advancing the ball past the midcourt line for almost four minutes at the start of the game. They had a fine team but were stymied by this unusual defense.

High school teams can win most of their games with the overplay-pressure man-to-man defensive system. It's a defense that also teaches individual and team pride. It forces the opponent's offense into unwarranted mistakes and then turns those mistakes into scores for the defense. Hard work, all-out effort, and pride are the necessary ingredients in order for the overplay-pressure defenses to work successfully.

A high school program that is based around this ball-hawking defense is going to be successful. Also, those gifted players on your squad that have an eye towards a college career will be more ready than the hundreds of other high school seniors who didn't learn how to play the "Big D" for this more advanced level of competition. Since there will be less for the player to learn on the collegiate level, this will give him an edge on a brighter basketball future. Many collegiate players have played nothing but the straight zone defense on the high school level and find the transition to the collegiate man-to-man defenses too demanding. The player who learns the overplay-pressure defensive system understands how to play the game with intensity and how to improve his defensive weaknesses rather than camouflage them.

Certainly, this defensive system isn't an easy, get-rich scheme. Hard work is needed by both the players and the coaches. Nevertheless, the return is well worth the sacrifices in terms of teaching players what it takes to be a champion on the court, in the locker room, and in life itself. *Coaching Winning Basketball with the Overplay-Pressure Defense* is a defensive program that you can take great personal satisfaction in teaching.

Ken Johnson

Contents

Coaching Winning Basketball with the Overplay-Pressure Defense

1

Development of the Overplay-Pressure Defense

FUNDAMENTAL ADVANTAGES OVER OTHER TYPES OF DEFENSE

Your Philosophy

Every coach should have a basketball philosophy that he truly believes will bring success to his players. Some coaches base their philosophy on the fast break and attempt to outscore their opponents. Others may base their philosophy on totally controlling the offense and playing at an extremely deliberate pace. We believe that a good basketball philosophy should be based on the style of team defense that is played. This should especially pertain to the high school coach who, from year to year, may not always have players who are skilled in all the offensive techniques. Even the outstanding offensive teams are going to have those games when the ball won't go through the basket, and they'll need a miracle to win.

Defense is the phase of basketball that with a great amount of work can be consistently excellent. The coach and the players are more in control here with a good defensive plan, than in any of the various offensive phases. The players must concentrate only on moving their bodies and not worry about moving with the ball.

What is the best type of defense from which to develop a sound basketball philosophy? We believe in a man-to-man type defense, with pressure techniques and strategies as described in this book.

The Zones

There are several traditional zone defenses like the 2-3, 1-2-2, 1-3-1, or the 3-2. These defenses may not, however, stop good offensive teams night after night. Over a period of time the offense can wear down the zone defensive players with good, disciplined passing and shoot the easy 10 to 15-foot jump shot at will. Even if the defensive team is in superb condition, they won't always be able to stop a quick-passing team from getting high percentage shots at the basket.

Teams that utilize traditional zone defenses to a great extent have a tendency to rest on defense at moments and as a result become less aggressive in the all-important rebounding phase of the game. Furthermore, this type of defense does not allow for any pressure to be applied to the offensive team that would help force bad passes or hurried shots.

Half-court and full-court zone presses are aggressive-type defenses that attempt to force the offensive team into hurried shots and forced passes. These have definite advantages. There are always two players trapping the ball, two players anticipating the next pass, and one player defending the basket. However, a good passing team that moves to the open areas and that believes in attacking the basket usually can be quite successful against this type of defense. Most of the zone presses are 1-2-2, 1-3-1, 2-1-2, or 2-2-1 set types. An alert coach will position his players in strategic areas against each zone and, thus, be extremely successful in getting a good selection of shots for his team.

The match-up zone defense is an excellent defense for smothering shots and gaining rebound position. It is extremely effective against offensive teams that attempt to move the ball, but doesn't attempt to cut players through the zone.

It is our feeling that the match-up is the most effective zone defense. Although it is still a zone defense that attempts to match up their players and set types against the offense, crisp passing, aggressive cutting from strong side-weak side and weak side-strong side, cutting to high post-low post, and baseline movement, may yield the open jump shot that the offense wants. Very few turnovers will be forced because it is not a pressure-type defense. It is more of a containment-type defense that attempts to get the offense standing and hesitating.

Flexibility of the Overplay Man-Man

The half-court man-man overplay of the Confusion Defensive System can do everything that traditional zones, zone presses, and match-up defenses can do, plus a little extra. It allows the defense better rebounding position because each offensive player may be screened away from the basket on every shot. The zone defense sometimes has difficulty in stopping a good weakside offensive rebounder because the defense is shifting to the ball movement. The man-man overplay defense can force bad passes, poor shot selection, and it is adjustable to the strengths and weaknesses of the opponents.

If the opposition is an outstanding outside shooting team, the man-man overplay-pressure defense will limit the effectiveness of these shots. Pressure will be applied at all times to the ball handler, and the passing lanes will be covered by the off-ball defenders. Thus, very few unmolested shots and passes could be attempted. If the offensive team has a strong inside game but a weak outside game, this man-man overplay-pressure defense may be relaxed to allow the offensive team more freedom on the perimeter and less freedom in passing the ball towards the basket. Any combination of pressure and non-pressure defensive positions may be taken by the defenders in order to adjust to the talent of the offensive team.

The man-man defense can be pushed to the full-court level in order to step up the tempo of the game. The man-man full-court pressure defense may be played straight-up, with the in-bounds double team, with the floater, or with the defenders playing face-up denial allowing the backdoor cut. Man-man overplay-pressure double-team techniques may be used in order to make it more difficult for the offense to advance the ball up the floor.

Diagrams 1-1 through 1-4 show the possible man-man overplay-pressure defensive adjustments in terms of positioning that are possible at the half-court level. Diagrams 1-5 through 1-8 show the possible full-court man-man overplay-pressure alignments.

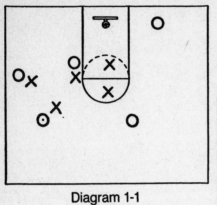

Diagram 1-1

Overplay Two-Man Sag

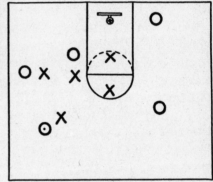

Diagram 1-2

Total Sag

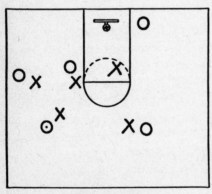

Diagram 1-3

Overplay One-Man Sag

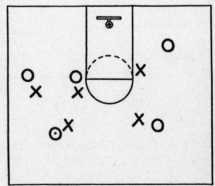

Diagram 1-4

Five-Man Overplay

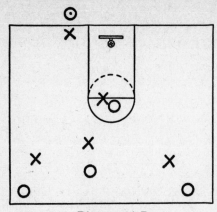

Diagram 1-5

*Man-Man Pressure Full-Court
Straight-Up Defense*

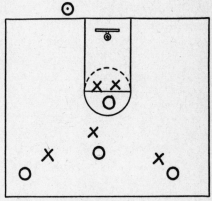

Diagram 1-6

*Man-Man Pressure Full-Court
with Double Team*

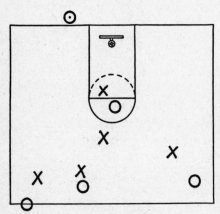

Diagram 1-7

*Man-Man Pressure Full-Court
with Floater*

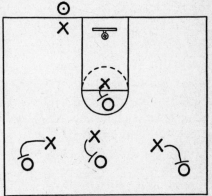

Diagram 1-8

*Man-Man Pressure Full-Court
Face-Up*

COACHING-LEVEL ASSIGNMENTS IN BUILDING
THE SYSTEM

Building a Program

At Hinsdale Central High School we initially used the Confusion Overplay-Pressure Defenses in building a successful basketball program into a winning situation. Our high school had enjoyed only one winning season during the previous eight years before my head coaching assignment was made. At age 24, I was a little apprehensive about managing the basketball program of such a large high school. With the encouragement of a fine athletic director, principal, and staff, we began the rebuilding task.

Having played basketball on the collegiate level and coached high school basketball on the freshman and sophomore levels, I had formulated some positive coaching ideas. My father was a member of the Illinois Basketball Coaches' Hall of Fame and my two brothers were also in the high school coaching ranks. Between my playing experience, coaching experience, and family background, years of basketball knowledge were at my disposal.

We began our program by opening the gymnasium for free play after school, prior to the beginning of the official playing season. Only four students participated. Obviously, basketball was not the popular thing to do at our school. We were now acutely aware of the challenge facing us. After years of constantly losing, the student body had literally given up on ever being competitive in basketball. Hinsdale had been extremely successful on the state and national levels in other sports, but not in basketball. Many fine athletes were shunning the sport. In some situations we realized that parents were discouraging their child from participating on the basketball squad because they wanted to avoid the anguish their child would suffer by participating in such a hopeless situation.

Underclass Coaching Experience

Every coach should have some experience on the freshman and sophomore levels of competition before testing the waters with a varsity team. Fortunately, I had experienced lower level coaching and had developed an understanding of the problems that the underclass coach faces and the unique role that he needs to play in order to benefit the overall program.

The varsity team is only as fundamentally sound as the underclass coaches can make it in the early teaching phases. The ninth and tenth grade teams must prepare fundamentally for the day on which they take the floor to compete as a varsity squad. The underclass coaches are present to teach these young players the proper way to play basketball physically, and the proper way to approach the game psychologically. It is very possible for the underclass coach to be successful with mediocre talent by using zone presses, combination defenses, and zone defenses. The coach may be winning the game, but the players are actually losing the war. Rather than teach fundamentals that they will need in future years as varsity players, the coach is shirking his duties by playing defenses that ninth and tenth grade players are not physically mature enough to beat. The coach's duty is to give his underclass players the best basketball education possible. He should let winning take care of itself. After all, the ultimate goal should be a winning varsity team, which is a direct result of effective underclass training.

Before that first season, we met with the entire basketball staff and installed the confusion half-court man-man overplay-pressure defense on all levels of competition: freshman, sophomore, and varsity. If a team does not establish a strong man-man overplay half-court defense, they may as well forget about the many additions and combinations that could complement this outstanding defense.

Once the season began, our coaching staff worked feverishly in teaching the fundamentals of this defense. Seventy percent of our practice time at each level was spent on the development of defensive fundamentals. The players were forced to move, to act and react, and to dedicate themselves to playing defense no matter what their physical limitations. Defense was the basis for our basketball philosophy. We were not teaching a conservative style of man-man. The coaches were encouraging the players to be aggressive, intense, and to attack the offensive team with such ferocity as to actually force them away from the basket.

Freshmen Level

Our freshmen coaches made specific contributions to the total program. These men were the most important people on our staff. Theirs was the initial impression that our staff would make on each player entering the program. The freshmen coaches helped to set the attitudes that the players would carry during their four years in our basketball program.

The following impressions or concepts were deemed important:

1. Impress on the players the need to go all out when playing.
2. Impress on the players that hard work in and out of the season will result in success for the team and the athlete.
3. Impress on the players the need to be proud of the effort they put forth.
4. Impress on the players the need for mental self-discipline.
5. Impress on the players the value of self-improvement—no matter what one's specific team status is.

The following skills would be stressed for teaching:

1. Teach individual footwork movement and other skills in the one-one situation.
2. Teach individual footwork movement and other skills in two-two situations.
3. Teach individual footwork movement and other skills in three-three situations.
4. Teach denial of passing lane skills.
5. Teach total five-man overplay denial skills with one-man sag.

When the freshmen team pressed, they used the straight man-man overplay position press with no double-teaming. It was simply a man-man overplay-pressure defense at the full-court level. This press was used to help teach aggressiveness and proved extremely valuable in doing so.

Sophomore Level

The sophomore coaches took over where the freshmen staff left off. Their contributions were critical.

What impressions were to be made?

1. Reinforce the initial impressions as presented by the freshmen staff.
2. Impress on the player the need for group reliance.
3. Impress in the players' minds their role in the total program.
4. Impress on the players the need for a strong body.
5. Impress on the players the need for a feeling of team pride.

What skills were to be taught?

1. Teach a constant review of individual techniques taught on the freshmen level.
2. Teach team defense with one- and two-man sag.
3. Teach team defensive help.
4. Teach exploitation of the offensive team's weaknesses.
5. Teach double-teaming techniques (no zones or zone presses).

Varsity Level

Once the players reached the varsity level, it was up to the head coach and his assistant to reinforce everything that had been taught by the freshmen and sophomore coaches. The man-man overplay-pressure defense needed to be executed 65 to 70 percent of the total practice time. Zones and zone presses were added in case of a specific need during a game. We would not, however, sacrifice a lack of sharpness with the man-man by spending too much time on the zone defenses. The zone defenses were sparingly used as a complement to the confusion man-man overplay defense. Ninety percent of our time was spent on the half-court man-man pressure defense. This defense must be the program's main staple if it is to build a consistently successful defense.

As varsity coaches, we played the man-man overplay-pressure confusion defense against all our opponents. The offensive abilities of a player can improve, but not to the degree of the defensive skills. This is a phase in which everyone, with the proper dedication and mental motivation, can be a contributing factor to the team's success. Although one player might be better at this phase than another because of natural talent such as extraordinary quickness, agility, or strength, everyone can learn and accomplish the basic positioning techniques fundamental to the confusion overplay man-man defense.

Rarely did we face a defense as tenacious as the one our players on offense practiced against each night. It was made clear to each team member that a real basketball player proves himself on defense, for this is the phase of the game in which the coach can see how badly a player wants to participate. Courage and determination are the necessary ingredients of a good defensive player. It's fun to shoot the basketball, but it's work to play without it. Defense is where our team's character is built.

An important advantage was that our offensive skills improved daily because of the tough defense that was played in practice. Our offense played with confidence during games because they knew the defense that they would face was not going to be as challenging as our practice defense. We were a better offensive team because of the Confusion Defensive System.

Pride of achievement became the goal of each defensive player. The idea of stopping one's offensive man and giving defensive help to one's teammates became the central theme of our team. It became a test of each defensive player's courage to see how difficult things could be made for the offense. Defense became a way of showing how much "heart" each player had. We announced to the team that the five best defensive players would start at each position. Usually, this meant that the five best all-around players on the team would start. More often than not, they possessed those abilities needed to be outstanding defensive players. No matter who started, all our players played their hardest because they realized that we meant what we said. Hustle, desire, and determination became the best adjectives for describing our team.

What were the impressions to be made?

1. Impress on the players the need for team pride in holding the offense to less than fifty points.
2. Impress on the players the need for total concentration.
3. Impress on the players the need for learning from one's mistakes rather than worrying about them.
4. Impress on the players an optimistic attitude toward life.
5. Impress on the players the need for team pride in giving everything as a 15-man unit.

What skills were to be taught?

1. Defending the cutting lanes.
2. Defending the floor angles.
3. Defending the basket situation.
4. Rebounding techniques.
5. Reviewing of individual skills.

The First Season

Our season began successfully. We weren't dynamic on offense that first year because we didn't have any great shooters, but our defense was tenacious. The players gave everything they had in terms of hustle and determination. We lost our opening game in overtime to the defending state champions and then won seven in a row. The team believed in the Confusion Defensive System, and we were well on our way to a winning season. The players realized that a tenacious defense could keep them on the floor with teams that had superior offensive firepower. Most of the opposition that year had not experienced such an intense defense.

Once our players learned the proper defensive techniques, they became "cannibals" with this half-court defense. The more success that each player met with, the more intensely he applied the overplay. The opposition became very frustrated when attempting to execute their patterns. Our defenders took away the cutting lanes, forced their offense further from the basket than normal, contested all passes, contested movement via the dribble, harassed the shooter, and screened out on the defensive boards. Once the opposition approached the ten-second line, they were about to enter a combat zone. Our defense conceded absolutely nothing to the offensive team. They were unable to withstand the effort that our players gave with the confusion overplay man-man defense.

In seven years of coaching at Hinsdale Central High School our overall record was 110-42. A clawing defense called "confusion" and some players who wanted to prove their worth as people were the reasons for this success.

Starting the System Again

Our second coaching position was an even more difficult job. We were told that this school was a "graveyard" for basketball coaches. They said the talent just wasn't there, but many times adults underestimate the character of today's young people. Larkin High School was a three-year school, which made it extremely difficult to install our Confusion Defense as previously explained. We went to work, however, with the aid of some fine assistants.

The first season was played basically with a junior-laden team that had finished toward the bottom of the sophomore league the previous year. We had an extremely inexperienced squad with which to work. They lacked a great deal of self-confidence in their ability to win. Long hours were spent on our half-court man-man overplay confusion defense, and we made a competitive showing.

During the season we could see the players growing in every phase of the game. Unfortunately, we couldn't seem to win. Twelve times we went into the last 90 seconds either tied or ahead—only to lose another game because of a fundamental mistake. It was frustrating for all of us, but the players never quit hustling. As the season drew to a close, we could see our players maturing as people as well as athletes. We were pleased with our first season even though 19 games were lost. The players were also pleased with this outcome. After our final loss, the locker room was filled with tears because there would be no more games and no more practices until the following November. One by one, the players came to our office and voiced their feelings.

"Coach, if we only knew at the beginning of the season what we know now, we could have been 19-6," said one player.

"I wish we could start the season tomorrow; we're ready. We know how to win now," said another.

These were strange comments for team members who had just lost 19 of 25 games, but we really hadn't had a losing season. It was a learning season. A season to learn about defense, basketball, and how to win. It was also a season to learn about ourselves as people and how to give of ourselves.

Before we knew it, the new season was upon us. Twenty-one victories were recorded by the same group that had won only six games the previous winter. They became the first 20-game winner in the school's history and had a banner year. The Confusion Defensive System works.

As has been said earlier in this chapter, *the Confusion Defense must be built on an outstanding man-man overplay-pressure defense.*

Some fine defenses on the collegiate level that are based on the man-man have been Bob Knight's defense at the University of Indiana, or Bill Cofield's at the University of Wisconsin. Another outstanding defensive coach is Dick Motta of the NBA. These defenses are ones that challenge the offensive team's every move.

GOALS OF THIS TYPE OF DEFENSE

Some general goals of the man-man half-court overplay defensive phase of the Confusion System are

1. To attain a healthy, competitive attitude among the players

2. To allow the players the opportunity to give an all-out effort

3. To allow each player the opportunity to be a contributing member of a successful program

4. To control the areas of the floor most often designated as areas of strength for the offenses in general, while being protective in all areas

5. To have extreme flexibility in the defensive alignment while never having to change actual assignments

6. To be able to get the basketball when necessary

7. To be able to control the pace and tempo of the game at the time when you don't have control of the ball

8. To control the movement of the offense

9. To establish absolute supremacy by proper positioning on the defensive board

10. To eliminate the uncontested and high percentage shot

11. To be able to force each offensive player away from his personal strengths

12. To psych-out the opposition

13. To build team pride

14. To build individual pride

OVERVIEW OF THE COMPLETE SYSTEM

One season it was my pleasure to coach an extremely gifted group of basketball players. The front-line players averaged 6'7" and were very mobile, rugged performers. The backcourt combination was outstanding: both guards were quick, intelligent players averaging 6'0" in height. This team was ranked by both wire services as one of the two best teams in the state of Illinois.

As the season progressed, teams began to slow down the tempo of our games. Eventually, when our opponents began using stalling tactics, we were faced with a difficult situation. With seven weeks still remaining before the state play-offs, we were no longer getting the opportunity to develop our players to their greatest potential. Something had to be done.

We decided that our team had to attack the opposition's offense at the full-court level. After much thought, we decided that the conventional presses would be too easy for our opponents to conquer. After all, they were simply trying to control the ball on offense and were not necessarily attacking the basket. They were playing a game of "keep away" with us. We needed to capture the ball in order to play and improve.

We decided to combine the man-man, 1-2-2, and 2-2-1 presses and the half-court man-man pressure defense into a total defensive concept. We went after the ball and created confusion for the opposition by concealing our defense. Much of the time the offensive players did not understand what type of defense they were facing. Our Confusion Defensive System often changed its defensive character as many as three times while the offense advanced the ball.

Some of our players refer to the press as a gang press! In one game we prevented a fine team from crossing the ten-second line for the first three minutes of the third quarter.

The most important aspects of the confusion press are our man-man press and man-man half-court pressure defenses. Sixty percent of the time we operate in the man-man press. Whenever the opponents hurt our combination presses, we come back to the man-man defenses.

2

Attacking the Offense with the Overplay-Pressure Defense

USING THE SCOUTING REPORT

There are four seconds remaining in the game between Genoa and Logan High Schools. Logan is trailing 52-50 with Genoa controlling the ball in a stalling offense, refusing to attempt a shot. The Logan coach signals his players to foul player #24 in hope that he'll miss the foul shot and turn the ball over to Logan High School for an opportunity to tie the game. Player #24 has only scored two points the entire game, and the Logan coach feels that he must be Genoa's poorest shooter. Player #24 makes the free throw to seal the victory for Genoa High School.

It's unfortunate that the Logan High School coach did not scout Genoa in their previous game. He would have discovered that #24 shot all of Genoa's technical free throws and was a fine shooter if given time to set.

The many values of a detailed scouting report are too often ignored. We feel a good scouting report can spell the difference between victory or defeat for our team. This is especially true when the other coach has the advantage of playing more talented players than our own. A good scouting report can be the equalizer. When your team is the underdog, you will need every possible edge in order to win. The more information you can impart to your players the better prepared they will be. The only pitfall is in how this information is presented. Your words should be selected with an unusual amount of care to avoid painting a mental picture of a "super-human" opponent. Instead, the players should appreciate their opponent's ability but feel that victory is theirs if the game plan, derived in part by a scouting report, is followed.

Scouting Report Values

The game plan evolves from the scouting reports. When making out our scouting schedule at the beginning of the season, we scout each opponent at least twice and if possible, even more. Our scout is a person familiar with our team's strengths and weaknesses, which aids us immensely in matching our talent against that of the opponent's, strategy-wise. The ultimate goal of our scout is to be as knowledgeable about the opponent as we coaches are about our own teams.

Another value of a detailed scouting report is that of self-evaluation. When working with our team day after day, we sometimes begin to over-evaluate or under-evaluate our talent. Because a coach becomes emotionally involved with his team, he may inadvertently make some coaching errors in the handling of his team. The wise coach will have his own team scouted by an outside evaluator periodically throughout the season. This outside evaluator should be someone the coach knows and trusts. Over the years these periodic self-evaluative scouting reports have proved invaluable to the overall improvement of our team. Many valuable ideas have evolved because the outside evaluator sees our team in a completely different perspective from the day-to-day contact of our coaching staff.

The scouting report form that we use is well detailed and asks some probing questions of the evaluator. Whether the person doing the scouting is experienced or inexperienced in the art of team evaluation, the questions help lead him into areas we feel are of major concern. The scouting report form does allow the evaluator, who is experienced, a large amount of latitude in expressing his thoughts in the report. Most high school coaches know the difficulty in finding qualified people to act as scouts. Thus, a well-detailed report can only help improve the quality of knowledge that we are seeking.

We ask the person doing the evaluating to write very little during the action of the game. We want the evaluator or scout to see the entire game and write only during breaks in the action and at the conclusion of the contest.

Our coaching staff watches the area papers for box scores and articles about our opponents. This gives us some knowledge of scoring averages, leading rebounders, leading percentage shooters, and in some cases we gain knowledge about offensive and defensive strategy from game articles. Our scout is then somewhat familiar with the opponents before he sees them play.

We take particular interest in players scoring from the field and foul line. We chart each player's performance game by game and watch for a pattern to develop. Some players score little but are excellent foul shooters. Some score well in all but the "big" games. Others rise to the occasion and play beyond their ability in important games. Box scores can give us valuable information if we take the time needed to do the recording.

Before our evaluator leaves to scout a game, we will impart what knowledge we have concerning the opposition and discuss areas of concern. We may also have various offensive and defensive strategies in mind for this particular opponent. All of this information should help the scout do a better job of evaluating the opposition.

Scouting Report Form Part I

Part I of the scouting report includes a page for player characterizations. Who are the starters and top substitutes? What are their heights and weights? What is their overall skill level? What positions do they play? What year in school are they? How many minutes does each play? This information may be jotted down before the game, during dead ball situations, and at the conclusion of the game. To get actual heights we tell our scouts to stand on the court near the players during pregame warm-ups. Many coaches list their players either taller or shorter than they actually are for various reasons. We want the exact heights. One coach listed his 6'8" center at 6'4" in the program.

Speed, quickness, agility and strength are elements of information that we are interested in under the title of skill level. Other needed information includes rebounding ability, shooting ability, ball-handling ability, and defensive ability. We want to know, specifically, how far from the basket each offensive player habitually establishes himself. We are interested in forcing each offensive player to operate from a spot initially farther from the basket than normal. We also tell our scout to watch each starter during pregame warm-ups in order to ascertain his favorite shooting area, shooting release, and shooting fakes. Often times our scout can determine the best way to defend each player's shot by watching during the warm-up periods.

Page 39 shows a replica of the lineup page used in the scouting report.

Scouting Report Form Part II

Part II of our scouting report form contains questions pertaining to the opponent's offense, full- and half-court diagrams for drawing plays, and note-taking pages. The questions dealing with the offense are structured to give a detailed description of the opponent's offensive tendencies. The following is a copy of those questions:

1. Do they use a continuity offensive pattern or simply execute a series of plays?
2. What are their most effective offensive cuts?
3. What is their offensive goal strategically?
4. What players dominate their offense and how?
5. How do they handle pressure at the half- and full-court levels?
6. How well do they rebound on the offensive board?
7. What type of ball-handling team are they?
8. Do they change anything when they substitute?
9. Should we attempt to speed up or slow down their offensive tempo?
10. How quickly do they make transitions from defense to offense?
11. How and when do they fast break?
12. When do they employ the delay game or stall?
13. What defense causes them the most trouble?
14. What is their level of physical conditioning?
15. How should we play them defensively?
16. Can you diagram all offensive sets and plays at the half- and full-court levels?

	No.	Ht.	Wt.	Min. Played	Skill Level Description
Forward—Yr.					
Forward—Yr.					
Center—Yr.					
Guard—Yr.					
Guard—Yr.					

Questions #1 and #2 probe the level of discipline that the opponents possess offensively. If they work the ball in a continuity pattern-type offense, we need to know that pattern and how often the ball is reversed to the weak side. Do they rely on options or special plays are executed out of the continuity offense? From what areas are the shots taken and off of what angle cuts? Once we know exactly where and in what direction the offensive cuts and shots are taken, we then make a concerted effort to break up the tempo of the opponent's movement or cuts.

If a team just runs designated plays, we need to know how they position their personnel, which players do the shooting, and what plays they execute. We also need to know what area of the court they are attempting to exploit. Are they a right- or left-handed team? All the informative questions about the continuity offenses also apply.

Question #3 deals with the coach's offensive philosophy in regard to player positioning and shot selection. Some teams attempt to spread the defense over a large area in order to penetrate via drives to the basket. They may run a weave-type offense waiting for the lane area to clear. This is most effective and can result in easy lay-ups if the defense is not prepared properly. Another strategy is to jam the defense into the lane in an attempt to free a player for the open 10-15 foot jump shot. Some teams look for the jump shot around the foul line, some concentrate on shots along the sides of the lane, and yet others like to exploit the baseline. All teams have a favorite shooting area. A 1-2-2 set offense will help force the defense inward because of the original position of the players before they begin to move. Many teams will run a pick-and-roll offense from this set. The passing game may be also run from a 1-2-2 or 2-1-2 formation and creates a great deal of movement by all five players in order to free a shooter for the high percentage jump shot. The shooter usually gets free by cutting off of a screen and towards the ball or basket, taking a 10-15 foot jump shot. The offense then helps determine the type of shots taken.

In question #4 we are concerned with their key players and how they are specifically used in the offense. We want to know what role each player fulfills in the team offense. We are concerned with our defensive match-ups. Our defender must know the characteristics and maneuvers that his offensive player possesses. He must have a feeling for his man after reading or hearing the scouting report. As well as knowing his man's offensive maneuvers, he must understand the man's level of quickness, speed, strength, and jumping ability.

Question #5 should help us decide the type of half-court or full-court pressure we will be able to use against them. Do we use a three-, four-, or five-man overplay at the half-court level? Would a half-court zone press be more effective? Should we vary our pressure? Is three-quarter court pressure or full-court pressure best? Should we vary the levels and types of pressure?

Question #6 should reveal the opponent's offensive rebounding methods. We will want to learn exactly how many of their players go to the offensive backboard. Once we know who their rebounders are, we would then be able to determine how to screen them away from the basket. Do they rebound with all five players or just the front line players? Do the opponents tip on the offensive board or go for complete possession? Do they work hard for inside position? Do they cover the foul line for the long rebound? What type of break can we run from our defensive board? Different fast breaks that we like to run after a defensive rebound would be the tipping break, designated flyer break, or control break. The type of fast break that we run depends on how well we can keep the opponents from getting the second and third shots.

Question #7 is interrelated with some previous questions. We want to know if the opponents attack best off of the dribble or the pass. Are they fluid ball handlers or are they mechanical? Are the dribblers proficient in moving both directions? Are they clever passers or are they prone to force passes and put their receivers in a position of disadvantage? Who is their best ball handler and how should we defense him?

Question #8 deals with the type of substitutes the opponents make as the game progresses. If a player does not start, it usually means that he has limited basketball ability in one or more areas. We need to know what his strengths and weaknesses are and how they effect the total offensive and defensive play of his team. We will make adjustments in order to take advantage of these limitations.

Some key questions for the scout to answer concerning a substitute player are:

1. Does the substitute improve or detract from his team's shooting ability?
2. Does the substitute improve or detract from his team's ball-handling ability?
3. Does the substitute improve or detract from his team's ability to control the offensive tempo?
4. Does the substitute improve or detract from his team's offensive rebounding?
5. Can the substitute handle pressure?

Tempo, an important key to every game, is discussed in question #9. The team that controls the tempo of the game usually holds the advantage. Some teams play their best basketball at a slow tempo or pace. Others perform best when participating in a quick-paced game. A large part of our defensive philosophy is based on not letting the offense do the things they do well. We attempt to force them away from their strengths as much as possible. We could never hope to beat a team with more talent than ours if we allowed them to play to their strengths. Thus, we hope to keep our opponents from getting into the flow of the game by controlling the tempo. Sometimes controlling the tempo means varying the pace of the game constantly. We've won some important games by playing to a slow tempo for several minutes, then abruptly quickening the pace for a few plays, and then returning to the slower tempo before the opponents can react. Tempo is controlled by the type of defense chosen that will encourage or discourage the opponents from adopting an early shot selection. Rebounding is also a key factor. Limiting the opponents to one shot is vital. Once they begin to play ping-pong on the offensive backboard your team is in serious trouble.

The transition game, as discussed in question #10, refers to the ability of the opponents to react as rapidly as possible from defense to offense. Some teams simply do not react well and can be beaten quite badly in this area. We are, of course, interested in how quickly the team reacts to the switch from offense to defense and from defense to offense, but we are also vitally concerned with how quickly the individual players react to the transition. For example, we may send a designated player down the court on a one-man fast break if we know his man is slow getting downcourt to play defense. We may also zone press in situations where we turn the ball over to the opponents on a missed shot if we know they are slow in filling their offensive positions.

Other information in question #10 that we are seeking is:

1. How quickly do they in bounds the basketball?
2. Who usually throws the inbounds pass?
3. How do they in bounds the ball against the full-court pressure?
4. Is their first reaction on a turnover recovery to pass or dribble?

Question #11 deals with the manner in which the opponents fast break after a defensive rebound. Some teams will break down the side of the floor, others will attempt to run the ball down the middle, and still others will attempt to fast break by throwing the long pass to a guard on a fly pattern.

We would prefer to find that the opponent fast breaks down the side of the court. Even though the ball can be quickly advanced up the floor, we feel that the passing lanes can be disrupted because they are predictable. The sideline fast break has limited options as compared to breaking down the middle. The sideline break can be better contained because of fewer offensive options. The sideline break curtails the effectiveness of the trailing play and cuts down the amount of passing angles to potential receivers. Because the ball is on the side of the court, the defense can jam the basket easier with the aid of the baseline. The options that the offense has will be in one direction. We should be able to put a considerable amount of pressure on the ball handler without having to defense as many reverse direction plays as a center lane break may initiate. Of course, the sideline break does have much merit and is a potent offensive weapon.

Most teams favor bringing the ball to the middle lane of the court either directly or indirectly and then filling both outside and trailing lanes. We want to know if the opponents have a designated ball handler to lead the break in the middle lane. We are concerned with where the ball is usually exited, which direction the rebounder turns in exiting the ball, what type of exit pass is thrown, how the rebounder copes with a double team, when the ball is dribbled, and any other tendencies the opposition may display in executing the fast break. Once all this information is gathered we may choose to fight the exit pass, play the passing lanes for interceptions, set ourselves in the fast-break lanes in an attempt to draw the charge, overplay the middle man or ball handler, or we may choose to simply retreat quickly and jam the basket to prevent the easy jump shot.

Question #12 deals with the stalling or delay tactics that the opposition employs. We believe in practicing against the other team's stall or delay before the actual contest. With the increasing use of the "four corner," a team must be prepared to do the best job of defending the delay game as possible. The delay game today is used by coaches at almost any point during a game, depending upon each coach's philosophy. The delay game has become an important offensive weapon, and the defense must be prepared to do the best they can to counter this control game.

We want to know the exact stalling pattern, how the opponent's personnel is used, who their poorer ball handlers are, when the best opportunity for a steal exists, where the offense should be pressured, how well they operate against traps, where the traps should be made, and which players are the poorest free throw shooters under pressure. We are interested in the scout's opinion concerning player match-ups, and the best type of defense to employ against the opponent's delay.

Question #13 refers to the type of defense that seems to give the scouted team the most trouble. (The key here is that we want to know *why*.) We are also extremely interested in the personnel of the team that played this defense against the scouted team. Did the team playing the defense have superior talent or was the defensive set responsible for the success against the scouted team? Are we capable of playing this defense?

Question #14 explores the level of the opponent's physical conditioning. Some teams have bulky players who often find it extremely difficult to play the entire game without becoming fatigued. This is usually more noticeable in the first half of the season.

Another important element that closely corresponds with physical conditioning is the amount of intensity or "heart" that a team shows on the court. We want to know the degree of effort the opponents put forth. Many times this alone determines our defensive plan and general game strategy.

If our scout feels that a team is not in the best physical condition, or that the opponent collectively does not play with a lot of intensity, we may press an entire game. Our press might not be effective until the final two minutes of the game, but we would gamble that in these waning moments our opposition will make a few critical errors and beat themselves. Total effort is what our team defense is based upon. A defense that is an outgrowth of a fierce competitive team attitude is what we are trying to attain.

Question #15 asks for the best type of defense to play versus the opponents. We are concerned also with player match-ups. It is important that the individual doing the scouting be familiar with our talent and style of play. He must realize that because of player limitations there are certain maneuvers that we cannot do defensively.

Scouting Report Form Part III

Part III of the scouting report form is a written evaluation of the opposition's coach. We want to know when he favors changing defenses or offenses. We want to know how he reacts to full- and half-court pressures. Does he use his time-outs selectively? Does he substitute for a strategic purpose? We are interested in anything that will help us understand the thinking of this coach, which in turn may assist in competing against him. For example, some coaches have a history of getting beaten by certain defenses. We want every edge possible when we go into the contest.

Part III also contains several player evaluation forms. We want to know all the characteristics of each offensive player to enable the defender to establish an excellent mental image of the type of player he will be guarding. Our defender will enter each contest with a game plan to assist him in containing his man.

Page 46 shows a copy of the player evaluation form.

Once the scouting report is completed, we go over the report thoroughly and prepare a game plan. We then present both the report and game plan to our team in a chalk session. We designate five players who will simulate the opponents during the week previous to the game. Our defense will work against the designated offense, learning a great deal about the intricacies involved in the opponent's attack. By the end of the week our defenders should have a very good feel for the opponent's every offensive move. Preparation is the key to victory and can help equalize the talent gap between two teams.

Player's Name   Yr.   No.   Pos.   Rh/Lh (Dominant Hand)

_____

Is he a driver, shooter, or both?

_____

How and where does he attack?

_____

What defensive abilities does he possess?

_____

How should he be defensed?

_____

What rebounding abilities does he possess?

_____

What is the level of his ball-handling ability?

_____

General Comments:

_____

ADJUSTING PRESSURE AREAS OF THE
DEFENSIVE ATTACK

After digesting the scouting report in its entirety, we determine the man-man pressure areas of our defensive attack. We may choose our 100 Pressure Defense, as shown in Diagram 2-1. This is a full-court man-man overplay-pressure defense. With this type of defense, we are denying all passes including the inbounds pass. The offense will be forced to advance the ball via the dribble. Our defender will be pressuring the dribbler all the way down the floor without allowing him to drive past for a penetration to the basket. We are attempting to continually force the dribbler to change directions and dribble the basketball with each hand. The defender is not necessarily attempting to steal the basketball as much as he wants the dribbler to mishandle it. Again, all passing lanes are denied.

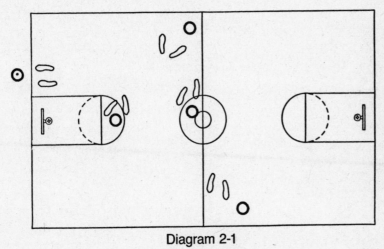

Diagram 2-1

100 Pressure Defense

Our 75 Pressure Defense is a three-quarter court man-man overplay-pressure defense beginning at our foul line as shown in Diagram 2-2. We allow the opponents to in bounds the ball and then use the same pressuring method as in the 100 Pressure once the dribbler advances to the three-quarter court mark.

Our 50 Pressure Defense is played from the midcourt line to our opponent's basket as shown in Diagram 2-3. In this style of man-man overplay-pressure defense we begin our pressure at the ten-second line in an attempt to force the opponent's offense further from the basket than usual. We want their initial setup positions pushed to the outside. This defense usually employs a five-man overplay, a four-man overplay, or a three-man overplay depending on our defensive strategy.

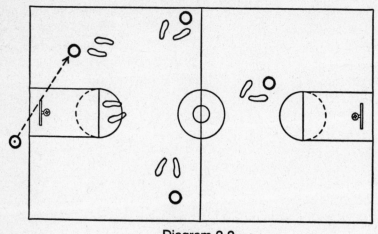

Diagram 2-2

75 Pressure Defense

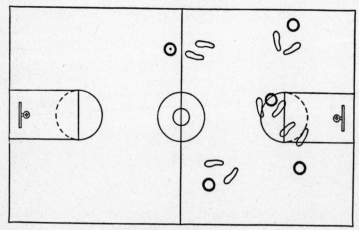

Diagram 2-3

50 Pressure Defense

The 25 Pressure Defense is played over the last quarter of the floor and allows us to heavily jam the weak side with as many as three defenders as shown in Diagram 2-4. The defense still pressures the ball and at least one strongside passing lane. The weak side of the defense is sagging towards the ball and basket much like a zone defense, yet maintaining man-man principles.

Varying these levels of pressure during a game may help to keep the offense from establishing a constant game tempo, therefore keeping them mentally off balance. At other times it may be best to go the entire game with one type of man-man overplay-pressure defense.

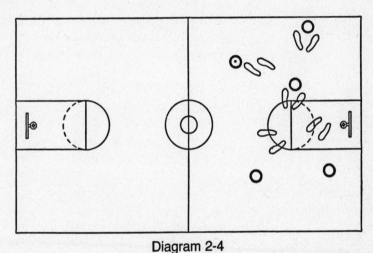

Diagram 2-4

25 Pressure Defense

ATTACKING THE TWO-GUARD FRONT OFFENSE

The two-guard front means that the opposition is using a 2-3 or 2-1-2 offensive set. Our scouting report should give us the exact set position of each player in the offense. Our first goal is to force each offensive player away from his normal setup position. We've found that most players get into the habit of setting up offensively on one specific part of the floor in relation to the basket. If we can force each offensive player further from the basket than normal, this will help cause disorientation for the player and the entire offense. The passes will be different, and the shooting areas will be different. Usually a player will have no difficulty in setting up in the correct offensive positions during practice. He then gets accustomed to operating offensively from a specific spot or area. It gets to the point that he instinctively knows where he is in relationship to the basket without looking. It is important that we not allow him this luxury. We will attempt to establish our defensive position in his favorite area quickly, and pressure him away from the basket by overplaying his passing lane aggressively.

The next area of interest is to learn the continuity pattern or plays the opponents execute. We will attempt to step into all cutting lanes and force the offensive players to alter their cutting routes. This will disrupt their offensive tempo and help disorganize them as a unit. In practice the opposition has probably been allowed to run their offensive cuts the exact way they are diagramed. If so, they are developing a definite offensive tempo. We must change the timing and angles of their cuts. This will aid in disrupting their shot selection and also cause them even more offensive problems. The opponents may have the basketball, but our defense will be controlling to a certain extent what they can do with it.

We will also choose the type of man-man overplay-pressure defense to play. Will we use a five-man, four-man, three-man, or two-man overplay-pressure defense? Will we use the 100, 75, 50, or 25 man-man pressure level?

The next area of concern is where we will try to funnel the basketball. Should we have our guards and forwards force the ball to the middle or to the sides of the court? Another option would be to play the dribbler "honest" and attempt to force a reverse-direction dribble, which might cause a ball-handling mistake. This will depend on the strength of our defensive pivot and the overall defensive ability of our team as compared to the offensive strengths of the opponents. We will adjust our pressure whenever necessary.

The one technique that we constantly employ in defending the 2-3 offense is denial of the pass to the strongside forward. Most offensive plays seem to be initiated with a pass to this man when the 2-3 or 2-1-2 sets are used. At all costs, we will take this pass away at the risk of weakening our defense somewhere else. If this pass is completed, we would then work especially hard at preventing the next pass from going into the post man. This would probably involve fronting the pivot man in most cases. Whether or not we will allow the pass to be returned to the strongside guard will depend on our strategy for that game. We prefer to use the three-man overplay on the strong side and have our weakside defenders jamming heavily toward the strong side and yet staying in the passing lanes to their men as shown in Diagrams 2-5 and 2-6.

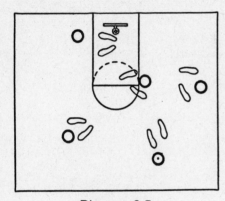

Diagram 2-5

Three-Man Overplay-Pressure Defense

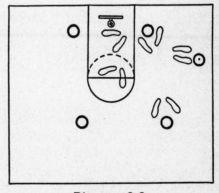

Diagram 2-6:

Three-Man Overplay-Pressure with the Ball at the Forward Position

ATTACKING THE 1-3-1 OFFENSE

Our basic man-man philosophy does not differ in its application against the two-guard offensive front and the one-guard front. Against the 1-3-1 offensive set, as shown in Diagrams 2-7 and 2-8, we will attempt to keep the point guard working hard in his attempt to handle the basketball and direct the offensive attack. We usually overplay the strongside wing man, forcing him to backdoor cut. The 1-3-1 affords the defense a baseline defender as well as a defensive pivot who can help stop the pass to the backdoor cutter. We will deny the ball to the pivot player in most situations unless the scouting report indicates we should not do so. Our major goal is to destroy the offensive tempo as previously discussed.

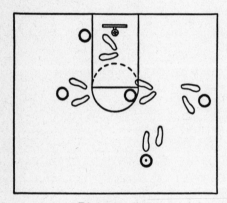

Diagram 2-7

1-3-1 Defensive Set

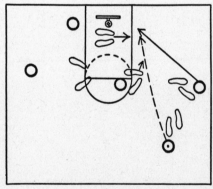

Diagram 2-8

*Defending the Backdoor Cut in
the 1-3-1 Set*

ATTACKING THE 1-2-2 OFFENSE

The 1-2-2 offensive set, shown in Diagram 2-9, is unique in that it lends itself to a great deal of dribbling and oftentimes proves to be a screen-and-roll offense. We want the same amount of knowledge about this offense as we needed in defending the two-guard front. We also use the same principles to disrupt tempo.

If it is indeed a screen-and-roll offense, we feel that it is imperative to pressure the point guard tenaciously in order to force him away from the usual double picks or screens that often await the defender near the top of the key, as shown in Diagram 2-10. In defending this offense we primarily want our defender to force the dribbler wide of the screen; therefore, he would slide

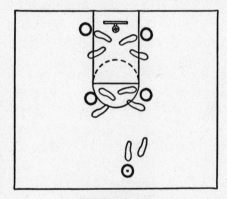

Diagram 2-9

1-2-2 Defensive Set

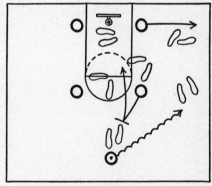

Diagram 2-10

*Fighting Over Top of Screen
and Defending Low-Post Cut*

over the top of the screen to negate its effectiveness. Another choice would be to slide behind the screen or pick and then quickly return to the dribbler. Another option would be to have our player switch or jump switch on such screens. Again, we would rely on the scouting report to help determine our best option in defending the screen. Exerting tremendous pressure on the point guard will often negate the screen entirely. It is vital, however, to begin pressuring the point guard at the three-quarter court level or as soon as possible. In some situations it may be possible to prevent the good point guard from getting the basketball. This would certainly hurt the continuity of the offense.

In defending the high-post screens, we would overplay these men with extreme pressure, forcing them from their normal screening positions and further away from their usual setup positions. A determined overplay by these defenders will be of critical importance to the point defender and will help destroy the team work between the ball handler and the screeners. Diagram 2-9 shows good defensive pressure at the high- and low-post areas. The defenders guarding the low-post offensive players should be positioned towards the foul line approximately six feet or more from their men to help defend against the lob to the high-post men, and also to be in a better position to deny the low-post men the ball when they break to the outside, as shown in Diagram 2-10. A position halfway up the lane or further would be dependent upon where the man is in relation to the basket-

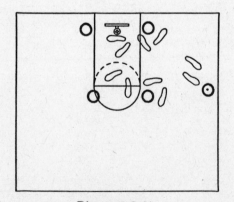

Diagram 2-11

Defending the Low Post

ball. The nearer the offensive player is to the ball, the tighter the defender would have to play him. This position by the low-post defenders of playing high in the lane certainly gives them an excellent angle to deny the pass on any cuts to the outside, but it also puts them in position to quickly front the low-post players when necessary, as shown in Diagrams 2-9 and 2-11.

ATTACKING THE PASSING GAME

The "passing game" as labeled by Bobby Knight, the Indiana University basketball coach, is extremely difficult to defend because of the perpetual movement and weakside screens constantly being used in this offense. It forces the defenders to be able to play defense at all possible positions. The defensive players are forced to display skills on a complete scale, rather than on a limited basis.

As a part of our defensive training, we have our defenders regularly practice against the passing game. We feel it helps improve our skills, plus it teaches our defenders alertness and intensity. A defender learns quickly never to relax or lose concentration.

The passing game can be run from either the 1-2-2 or 2-1-2 sets. We would prefer to defend the 1-2-2 passing game set if they aren't attempting to post our defenders near the basket. The 1-2-2 set would then be putting emphasis on the high percentage jump shot of less than 15 feet. The 2-1-2 passing game puts constant pressure on our inner defense because there is often a definite post player who is working to get the ball around the basket. Because of the movement of the other four players in the 2-1-2 or 2-3 sets, it is difficult to give weakside help to the low-post defender. It takes well-trained defensive players to be aware of their varying responsibilities as they shift from defensive guard, forward, and center positions on both the strong side and weak side of the court.

We have had a reasonable amount of success in defending the passing game because our players are taught all the different defensive skills used at each position and asked to play every defensive position, not just in our drills, but also in scrimmage situations. Our second unit executes various offenses to help our defenders improve their skills and knowledge of defensive positioning. We try to never enter a contest where our players are caught unaware of how to defense the opponent. We feel that by learning the proper defensive philosophy, principles, and skills that we'll be able to defend any type of surprise offense successfully. In other words, the man-man overplay-pressure defensive philosophy should cover all possible offensive situations.

In defending the passing game, we overplay all strongside passing lanes. We are overplaying all players who are one direct pass from the ball. It is important that the defender does not follow his man too tightly when he cuts away from the basketball to the weak side. The further the man cuts away from the ball, the more room we allow him in our attempt to anticipate his eventual return cut towards the ball or basket. The weakside defender should remain between his man and the basketball, with himself towards the middle of the floor, and favoring the strong side of the court. This will aid the defender in avoiding weakside screens, besides allowing him to easily maintain the overplay position when the offensive man makes his cut back to the ball. This type of positioning also allows the defender to give valuable weakside help against backdoor cuts from the strong side or against lobs into the post area.

The main objective of the defense is to destroy the rhythm of the opponent's cuts and passes. We don't want to get a step behind the cutters and allow uncontested passes to be thrown. If the defenders begin trailing the offensive cutters, the passing game will work to perfection.

Because of the unusual amount of movement the passing game affords its players, they may take shots with our guards caught at the forward and center positions. We work hard all season to develop good screening techniques to prevent the offense from getting second and third shots. It is vital that all of our defenders screen the offensive rebounders from the basket on every field goal attempt. Rebounding is critical to any defense. Without strong rebounding skills, a team is going to encounter serious problems.

ATTACKING THE WEAVE OFFENSE

The weave offense that we most commonly have to defend is the 1-3-1 dribble screen executed by three or four players with a screener operating from the high-post position. Diagrams 2-12 and 2-13 show this offense in operation.

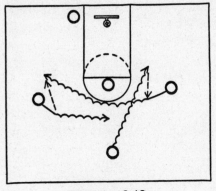

Diagram 2-12

Weave in 1-3-1 Set

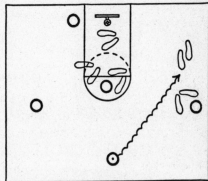

Diagram 2-13

Defending Handoff

The key to containing this offense is for the defenders to fight over the top of the dribble screen and prevent the handoff. This will quickly destroy the continuity of the offense. We also will overplay both wings and force them into backdoor cuts. Weakside defense will be needed to help defend these cuts. Our low-post and high-post defenders are positioned to help intercept all passes to backdoor cutters from the outside. If we can keep a great deal of pressure on the point man, and if the wing defenders recover quickly enough to help defend the backdoor cut, few passes to these cutters will be completed. Constant pressure resulting in the offensive team being forced further and further from the basket is the key in disrupting this or any other offense.

ATTACKING THE STALL

We feel that to be able to defend against the other team's stall is a critical part of any pregame preparation. There's no lonelier feeling in the world for a coach than to watch the opponents play "keep-away" with the ball when his team is behind by two points. What often happens is that the defense must foul the offense in order to have a chance to get the basketball. The problem, of course, is that the offense gets to shoot either one or two foul shots. If they are good shooters, the game is over. Here are some goals we have when the other team is stalling:

1. The defenders should force a five-second count and the jump situation by denying all passes.
2. The defenders should set up for the charging foul in the cutting lane.
3. The defenders should set up for the charging foul from the dribbler.
4. The defenders should force the ball toward the corners or midcourt line.
5. The defenders should double-team the ball whenever it is moved into one of the corners.
6. The defenders should double-team the ball on all handoffs.
7. The defenders should know the offensive pattern, if there is one, and take advantage of this knowledge.
8. The defender should fight every pass his man attempts to throw.
9. The defenders should double-team on all handoffs or screen-and-roll situations.
10. The defenders should attempt to foul the poorest foul shooter when all else has failed.

Defending the stall is a critical part of any game strategy. Being able to evaluate the opponent's coach via scouting reports should help prepare your team for the exact time that the opponents will employ the delay or stall. The advantage in having this information is that, mentally, the defenders will always be a step ahead of the offense. Thus, the defense will be able to react quickly to the change of the tempo. We also want to know what offensive stall pattern the opponents use because this gives us the edge in helping to attain the above mentioned goals. It will help us anticipate each opponent's usual offensive cut and increase the chance for an interception or offensive turnover.

MAJOR PRINCIPLES OF THE MAN-MAN OVERPLAY-PRESSURE DEFENSE

1. Don't allow the defensive guards to be split by the drive.
2. Don't allow the forward and guard to be split by the drive.
3. Don't allow the driver to penetrate along the baseline.
4. Force all cutters away from the ball and basket.
5. Front all players eight to ten feet from the basket.
6. Overplay the center at the high-post position.
7. If the ball goes inside, the defense should collapse around it, forcing a pass to the outside.
8. Overplay all passes to the strongside forward.
9. Overplay all passes to the strongside guard.
10. Overplay receivers who are one pass from the ball handler.
11. Turn the dribbler whenever possible.
12. Allow no uncontested shots.
13. Weakside defenders should favor the ball-side, yet remain in the overplay position.
14. Anticipate screens from the strong side to the weak side.
15. Always anticipate and deny cuts from the weak side to the strong side.
16. Attempt to draw the charging foul.
17. Communicate on defense.
18. Learn to use defensive floor angle positioning to the defender's advantage.
19. Double-team the dribbler when he turns his back, thus putting himself in a position of disadvantage.

20. Learn to fight over all screens as the first option.

21. When guarding the man without the ball, learn to see both the man and the basketball simultaneously.

22. Always attempt to anticipate the offensive man's next move and beat him to that spot.

23. Force the offense further from the basket than normal by a tenacious overplay.

24. Make the offensive man play to his weaknesses, not his strengths.

25. Screen each offensive man from the basket after every shot.

1st Quarter   *Defensive Chart Evaluator*

	Jeff	Dave	Greg	Chuck	Jim
1. Failure to anticipate					
2. Failure to use proper defensive stance					
3. Failure to use hands and arms properly					
4. Failure to fight pass with hands					
5. Failure to see man and ball					
6. Failure to use proper footwork					
7. Failure to use body properly					
8. Failure to stay on floor					
9. Failure to hold guarding distance					
10. Failure to deny offensive strengths					
11. Failure to collapse on ball at post					
12. Failure to front					
13. Failure to deny cut to ball					
14. Failure to deny cut to basket					
15. Failure to overplay					
16. Failure to defend baseline					

1ˢᵗ Quarter   *Defensive Chart Evaluator*

	Jeff	Dave	Greg	Chuck	Jim
17. Failure to turn dribbler					
18. Failure to contest shot					
19. Failure to jam from weak side					
20. Failure to deny split					
21. Failure to help on the backdoor pass					
22. Failure to defend free man					
23. Failure to sag					
24. Failure to use floor angles					
25. Failure to double-team					
26. Failure to cover up on double-team					
27. Failure to communicate					
28. Failure to go over the screen					
29. Failure to go behind the screen					
30. Failure to switch on the screen					
31. Failure to play hard or with intensity					
32. Failure to recover quickly					
33. Failure to box out					

The preceding chart on page 60 is used to help record each individual player's defensive performance during a game. We write the exact time of each defensive lapse in the appropriate square under the player's name. It gives each player a clear indicator of his weaknesses. The defender can go over the game mentally by himself or with his coach using this chart and recall the exact plays in question. He is better able to replay the game and analyze his defensive maneuvers with the aid of this chart.

We usually have one of our assistants do the recording. It is important for him to know the exact location of each item or he will become lost and confused. If possible, it is most advantageous to use a spotter and a recorder. This speeds up and simplifies the entire process.

3

Defining Individual
Defensive Assignments

At the beginning of every basketball season, we have approximately 21 practice sessions before our opening season tournament. We don't have the time necessary to develop defensive fundamentals to any degree of perfection. The bulk of our time is spent on team defensive organization, attempting to prepare for the type of offenses that we might encounter in this opening season tournament. After our preseason organizational sessions are completed, we accelerate with *great intensity* in teaching individual defensive fundamentals. Drill work is stressed. Therefore, we teach the whole, to part-to-whole method at the beginning of the season.

Once the season is established, our practice sessions change in their structural makeup. We begin with individual defensive drill situations for 30 to 40 minutes each day and then follow up with team defensive situations. We would then be using the part-to-whole method of learning. The methods of learning constantly vary as the season progresses, depending on our learning needs.

Let's discuss, position by position, the defensive assignments of each player.

Guard Play

The main objective of our guards is to force the offensive guards to relinquish their dribble as soon as possible. We want this to occur in a position of offensive disadvantage. Positions of disadvantage would be:

1. Just as the offensive guard crosses the ten-second line.
2. Just before the offensive guard crosses the ten-second line.

3. Just after the offensive guard reaches the "coffin corner" (that area at the intersecting point of the sideline and the ten-second line).

4. Just after the offensive guard reaches the 25-foot mark from the basket.

When the guards can force their men to pick up the dribble in any one of these four positions of disadvantage, the defensive team can really turn on the overplay pressure. Once the offensive guard gives up his dribble, the defender moves in close and attempts to fight the pass with his hands. The defender shadows the ball with his hands while in a wrestler's stance with the body weight distributed evenly on the balls of the feet. Even though the defensive guard is aggressively attempting to deflect the pass, he never leaves the floor. Once the defensive player has both feet in the air, the advantage immediately shifts to the offensive player. Three things are likely to happen when the defender recklessly leaves the floor—none of the three are acceptable:

1. The defensive player can bump the offensive player, creating a foul.

2. The defensive player can give up the passing lane by leaping into the air and out of position.

3. The defensive player can create an easy give-and-go situation for the offense by leaping out of position.

A player should only leap into the air when he knows that the offensive player has committed himself to either a shot or pass. Too often the defender, in his eagerness to help his team, leaps in reaction to an offensive fake. Having extraordinary leaping ability is a definite advantage in basketball, but the player must know how and when to use it.

How do we force the offensive guard to relinquish his dribble in a position of disadvantage?

We tell our defensive guards to attack the offensive guards at the three-quarter court mark. With defensive pressure beginning at this point, we can make it difficult for the offense to advance the ball toward their basket and not spread ourselves too thin, thus allowing an offensive guard penetration.

Our guards await their offensive counterparts in a wrestler's stance or a parallel stance. Once the ball-handling guard reaches the three-quarter court mark, we meet him with one-one pressure. Our defender moves from the parallel stance to a straddle stance as shown in Diagram 3-1.

The defender in Diagram 3-1 has dropped his left foot backwards and is using a straddle stance in guarding the dribbler. The defender's right foot splits the center of the dribbler and the left foot is positioned back and a half-body to the outside of the ball handler. The defender is an arm's length from his man and is sliding diagonally in order to prevent the dribbler from getting past.

When the ball handler reverses his dribble, as shown in Diagram 3-1, the defender pivots on his back foot (left) by sliding the front foot (right) backwards into the straddle position. He quickly shuffles ahead of the dribbler a half-body length and keeps pressure on his man.

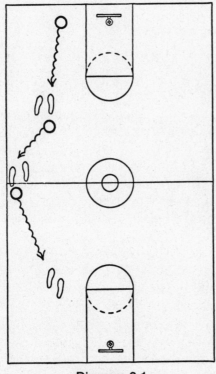

Diagram 3-1

Arm position is also crucial to the defender. If the right foot is the front or top foot, the right hand should be used in the up position to defend against a quick pass or shot. The left hand and arm are down and towards the ball in order to bat away or steal an errant dribble or pass. As the defender pivots into the straddle stance going to his right, the left arm and foot are forward, and the right hand and arm are back. The defender should keep his weight evenly distributed, knees flexed in an aggressive position, with the head and shoulders elevated slightly to promote balance and quickness.

Does the distance of the defender to the dribbler vary?

We would like the defensive man to be as close as possible to the dribbler without allowing himself to get beaten by a quick drive to the basket. Defender distance relationship to the ball handler then depends on the quickness and intelligence of the defender as compared to that of the offensive man. Scouting reports on the opposing players are extremely important when deciding personnel match-ups in the overplay-pressure man-man defense.

What is the basic objective of the defensive guards when defending the dribbler?

We would like our defensive guards to apply as much pressure as possible to the ball-handling guard. Our defensive guard is told to turn the dribbler as many times as possible before he can advance the basketball into the scoring area. Thus, the importance of our defender positioning a half-body to the outside of the dribbler is critical. He must turn the dribbler in the other direction and then establish body position again. Once the half-body outside positioning is established, the defender may force the dribbler to change directions again. This is not an easy task, and it involves much drill time in practice.

The danger of this turning maneuver is that the dribbler may get past the defender when he changes direction. If the defender continues to shuffle when making his reverse pivot after turning the dribbler, he will get beaten on the drive to the basket occasionally. Our players are told to pivot and then take two quick running steps ahead of the ball handler until they have regained their body positioning advantage. Once their body position has been regained, they may return to the shuffle or sliding movement.

Our defensive guards are very rarely beaten on the turn of direction by the dribbler. By being a half-body to the outside, the defender has the mental advantage of knowing what the dribbler's next logical move will be. We feel that 70 percent of defense is recovery, and this is just a recovery move to the defender's weak side. It is a move that he knows is coming; therefore, he can get a jump on the play because he has already eliminated half of the choices for the dribbler by using the outside half-body overplay position.

Never play the ball handler head-up or in an honest position, allowing him the opportunity to go in either direction. Take many of his opportunities away immediately by body positioning to one side or the other. The defender can then anticipate where the offensive player may attack and recover to that point. This is called *defensive anticipation* and is critical in order for each player to become a successful defensive player.

When recovering to a defender's weak side as the dribbler changes direction, our players are also told to pick a spot one or two yards ahead of the dribbler and beat him to that area. We call this playing the "angles of the floor." If the dribbler draws even to the defender and the half-body position is lost, we expect the defender to spring away and recover his body position by beating his man to an imaginary spot on the floor ahead of the dribbler. Far too many defenders are satisfied to ride on the hip of the dribbler. This usually results in the defender fouling the dribbler or getting beaten on the drive to the basket.

By forcing the dribbler to change directions several times, he will often give up his dribble too soon in order to escape the pressure of one-one harrassment from the defender. Many times the ball handler will find himself stranded near the midcourt line looking for a receiver. Once the opponent has given up his dribble, our defense goes into a complete denial of all offensive passing lanes. The defensive guard on the ball handler fights the pass vigorously. This often results in an errant pass that the defense can intercept. This type of pressure also pulls the offensive team farther from the basket, thus, negating to some extent the possible size advantage that they might hold. Diagram 3-2 shows this defensive situation.

The position of the defensive weakside guard is important. He is positioned about a step and a half toward the center of the court or toward the strong side and one step below the passing lane. He uses the straddle stance with the foot nearest the strong side of the court as the front foot. This is the normal straddle position. If the left foot is forward then the left arm is also forward, discouraging the pass to the weakside guard. The knees are flexed in an aggressive position with the head and shoulders slightly upward. The defender's weight should be evenly distributed throughout the feet. The weakside guard is always in position to intercept a sloppy or errant pass to his man.

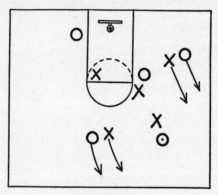

Diagram 3-2

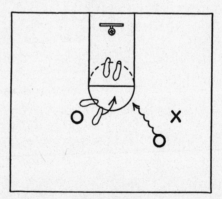

Diagram 3-3

It is also the responsibility of the weakside guard to make certain that the dribbler does not split the defensive guards with a quick drive to the basket. If the strongside defensive guard loses the dribbler, the weakside guard drops back to the center of the foul line or below, slowing down the penetration of the dribbler and keeping both offensive guards in front of him until the beaten defender can recover to one of the offensive guards. The defensive guards must never allow the dribbler to penetrate between them. The recovery movement is shown in Diagram 3-3.

In Diagram 3-3 the weakside guard used the reverse pivot on the left foot, sprinted or quickly shuffled to the foul line and assumed the wrestler's stance. He then attempts to read the play and determine if he must take the dribbler or if the strongside guard can recover quickly enough to avoid a switch in defensive assignments.

What are the duties of the strongside defensive forward?

The strongside forward positions himself to prevent his man from receiving a pass. The pass that is defended most often is the strongside guard-forward pass. Many offenses are initiated with this pass.

The strongside defensive forward is a full arm's length from, and on the ball-side of his man. In Diagram 3-4 the action is again taking place on the left side of the court.

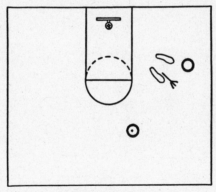

Diagram 3-4

The defender's right foot is perpendicular to and shy of the passing lane. Toeing the right foot in this manner helps open the shoulders and head, which allows the defender a better position from which to observe the basketball. When guarding the man without the ball, the defender must always see both his man and the basketball. He must never lose sight of either. His right arm and hand extend just into the passing lane. The defender's weight is evenly distributed throughout the feet with his knees flexed, his head and shoulders slightly upward. By keeping the head and shoulders slightly upward, the defender will maintain better balance and will also be able to see both the man and basketball easily. This will also greatly improve the defender's ability to react.

The defender is approximately one yard away and to the ball-side of the offensive forward. He should attempt to maintain this position until his man receives the basketball. Of course, the defender's obligation is not to allow his man the opportunity to receive the basketball. If the offensive player moves towards the ball, the defender must maintain his position in relation to his man as shown in Diagram 3-5.

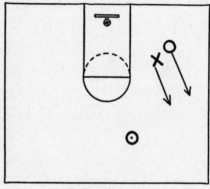

Diagram 3-5

What happens if the offensive forward backdoor cuts to the basket?

The defensive forward simply turns his body in the opposite direction, and using the same overplay position for denying the guard to forward pass, he defends the backdoor cut and pass. We call this turning of the body a "head snap." Diagrams 3-6A and 3-6B show this movement.

The defender keeps his chest facing his man and simply turns his head from the right shoulder to the left shoulder, assuming the same former guarding position, only now his movement is to the left. If the offensive forward gets too far ahead of the defender on the backdoor cut, the defensive man should sprint with hands up until he can recover his guarding position.

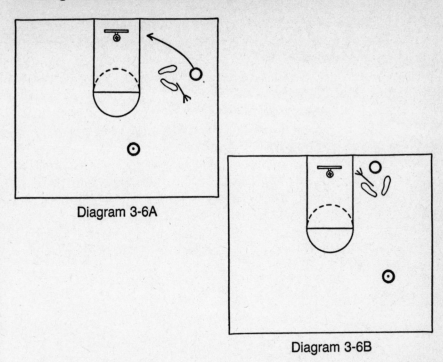

Diagram 3-6A

Diagram 3-6B

By putting his hands upwards over his head on this recovery move, the defender is making the passer lob the ball to the receiver. The defender may then have an opportunity to intercept or deflect this pass. Also, the man guarding the passer should be fighting this backdoor pass. We want the offensive forward to backdoor cut because we feel that this pass is extremely difficult to convert, and it also takes away from their offensive continuity. Our players spend much time in practicing our denial drills. Twenty or thirty minutes of each practice session are devoted to this task. Our defenders also spend much time in developing their recovery skills. Recovering to defense the backdoor cut is not as difficult as one might think. With the weakside defenders favoring the backdoor cutter and helping to discourage the lob pass, the recovery task of the strongside forward is made easier.

How does the defensive forward react when his man does receive the strongside pass?

As the offensive forward breaks out to receive the pass, the defender will immediately sense whether or not he can deny him this pass. If he knows that the offensive man has beaten him to the spot, he moves quickly away and to the baseline side of his man. The natural reaction of the pass receiver will be to drive in the opposite direction from which he has been constantly pressured. If the forward receives the pass from the guard, his move will be to drive the baseline away from the previous pressure. The defender must stop the baseline drive and turn him towards the middle. When the offensive player starts to advance towards the middle, the defender attempts to recover to a spot several feet ahead of him. Once he has regained his outside half-body ahead guarding position, he attempts to turn the dribbler again. The defender is attempting to force his man to give up the dribble. We've found that most offensive players will make two offensive moves and then pick up the basketball. Diagrams 3-7A, 3-7B, and 3-7C show the defensive footwork involved.

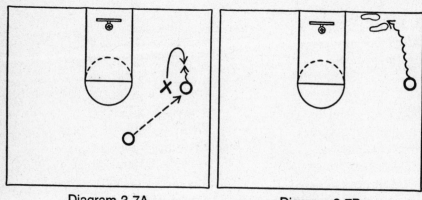

Diagram 3-7A   Diagram 3-7B

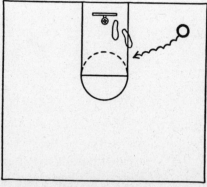

Diagram 3-7C

The defensive forward uses the same straddle stance that the guards utilize in defending the dribbler. When guarding the man with the basketball, all of our defenders employ a uniform stance.

Basically, we have been discussing the strategy used in guarding the man without the ball who is the primary receiver. The primary pass receiver is the man who is one pass from the ball. The same technique is employed by all our defenders when guarding the primary receiver. Let's turn our attention to defending the secondary receiver.

When guarding a secondary receiver, the defender should position himself between his man and the basketball. He should be about two full steps to the ball-side of the offensive player. The straddle stance should be used, and the body positioned so the basketball and offensive player may be seen at the same time by the defender. The basic positioning from the weakside forward slot is shown in Diagram 3-8.

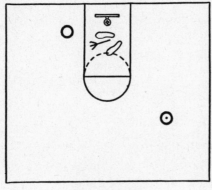

Diagram 3-8

By remaining in the above position the defender can prevent his man from cutting directly towards the basketball. If the lob pass is thrown over his head, the defender should recover the same way the strongside forward would on the backdoor cut. He sprints or shuffles toward his man using the "head snap" with his hands held high, attempting to deflect or intercept the pass. If good pressure is being maintained on the passer, very few of these lobs will be completed.

The defensive forward must also anticipate his man's weak-side movement. Obviously, the high-post cut is already covered because of the position of the defender in relation to the basketball. The cut that will probably be made is one to the strongside low post. The defender should be ready to move to that area. As the offensive man moves in to the primary receiving area, the defender adjusts to the tighter overplay position. The weakside forward should never be allowed to receive the ball in or near the lane area. Thus, it is vitally important that the weakside forward position himself directly between the man and the basketball at all times.

What is the position of the weakside guard when defending a secondary receiver?

The strongside forward has possession of the ball. Once again, like the weakside forward, the defender is directly between his man and the basketball. He shades toward the center of the lane waiting for his man to move towards the ball. He prevents the direct cut to the ball and anticipates a backdoor cut to the basket. The guard uses the "head snap" movement in defending the backdoor cut as previously described in our discussion of backdoor strongside forward defense. The defensive guard should not allow his man to receive the basketball in or around the lane area. Diagram 3-9 shows the weakside guard defensive position.

How does the center defend the post position?

The defensive center should always play on the ball-side of his man whenever possible. As long as the offensive center is in the pivot area, the defender must be an arm's length away, using the straddle stance with the hand and arm in the passing lane. It is critical that he prevent the ball from entering the pivot area. The weakside guard and forward will be able to help the defensive center with this assignment in various situations, but the basic responsibility lies with the defensive center.

Diagram 3-10 shows the defensive center position when the ball is at the guard position. If the guard passes to the forward, the defender must again move to the overplay position between the ball and his man. There are two ways to do this. First, he may use the "step across" method. In Diagram 3-11A the defender's right foot is forward. He steps across the front of the offensive man with the left foot and then follows with the right foot.

Therefore, he steps into the overplay position on the left side, with the left foot forward as shown in Diagram 3-11B.

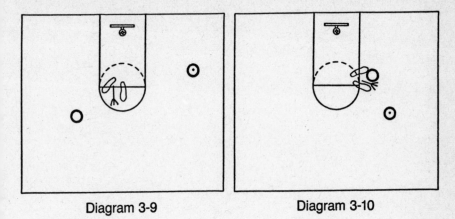

Diagram 3-9   Diagram 3-10

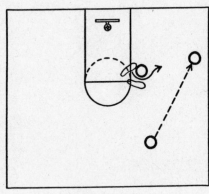
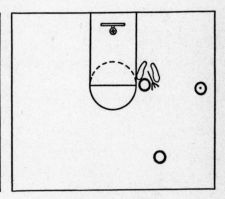

Diagram 3-11A   Diagram 3-11B

This is an excellent method if the defender is agile and able to react quickly. If not, we have the defender use the "slide behind" method. That is, he shuffles into the overplay position by moving behind and to the low-post side of the offensive center. Diagrams 3-12A and B show this defensive movement.

When the offensive center moves to the low post, our defender will front him within a radius of five to eight feet from the basket. If the offensive center moves to the weak side, our defender lets him go and plays him the same way as our weakside forward would play his man in an identical situation.

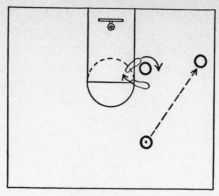

Diagram 3-12A

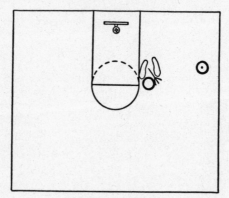

Diagram 3-12B

DEFENDING FLOOR ANGLES

Defending the floor angles is another concept that we teach our players. The defender, when guarding the man without the ball, is anticipating the cut to the basketball. Our defender denies this cut by positioning his body in the cutting or passing lane. Our defender will always favor the strong side of the floor. He never moves to the weak side of the floor to begin playing a tight overplay. He floats in the diagonal center of the half court anticipating the cut from the weak side to the strong side. By favoring the strong side he will have the better floor position. The cutter will usually make two steps before our defender must react. A defender must continually work at developing an understanding of his body position in relation to the man and the ball. If all cuts toward the basketball can be interrupted, the offensive timing of the opponent's offense will be ruined.

When guarding the man on the strong side, the defender should be in the overplay position so the offensive man can take one full step before he needs to react. If the offensive man has to take two full steps before he can get open, the defender should be able to adjust his body distance in relation to his man and deny him the ball. It is important for the defender to visualize where a step or two will move the offensive man. In his anticipation, the defender must be two or three steps ahead of the offensive man's potential cut, mentally. Diagram 3-13 shows the positioning in response to such a situation.

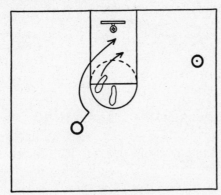

Diagram 3-13

The weakside guard is shown defending the cut to the ball and then to the basket. First, he stops the cut to the ball by being in the overplay position at the diagonal center, favoring the strong side and denying the passing lane to this secondary receiver. He then uses the head snap and maintains the overplay position on the backdoor cut to the basket. Usually, the cut will conclude at the strongside low post and then the offensive man will move away to the weak side.

Diagrams 3-14A and 3-14B show defensive reaction to the give-and-go cut. The defender is in the straddle stance attempting to turn the dribbler when the pass was entered to the strongside forward. The defender immediately moves away and to the outside in order to stop the direct cut to the basket. This puts the defender in the overplay position, and he simply uses the head snap when defending what becomes a backdoor cut.

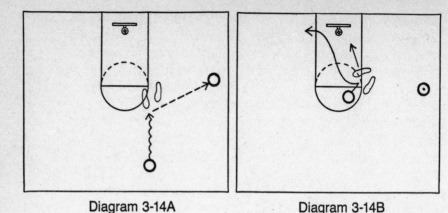

Diagram 3-14A   Diagram 3-14B

COVER-UP ASSIGNMENTS

Recovering from the Missed Interception

Whenever a defender is beaten by his man, he must make an all-out effort in an attempt to recover from his defensive lapse. In attempting to recover to a position of advantage, we instruct our players to recover towards the basket. The defender picks a spot on the floor several feet ahead of his man and outsprints him to this position between the offensive player and the basket. Diagrams 3-15A and 3-15B show this maneuver from the guard-to-forward pass and from the guard-to-guard pass.

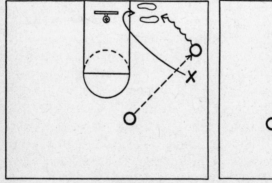

Diagram 3-15A   Diagram 3-15B

What happens when a defender is badly beaten on an offensive play by his man? Who will cover up until the beaten defender can hustle back into position?

The defensive player who has the primary duty of covering the open cutter charging towards the basket is the center. His defensive responsibilities are to defend the basket, to prevent the offensive center from handling the basketball, to prevent the backdoor passes, and to prevent open drives to the basket for lay-up shots. When he sees an open man cutting or dribbling towards the basket, he moves back towards the goal and keeps all the action in front of him until the other defenders can help. By moving directly in front of the basket, he can slow the driver and keep his own man from getting behind him for an easy lay-up. The defensive center should wait until the last possible instant before committing himself to the driver. By having the defensive center float in front of the goal and slowing down the play, the beaten defender may also be able to recover. Diagram 3-16 shows the cover-up positioning behind the beaten defender.

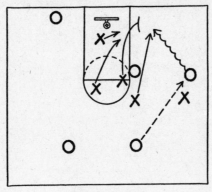

Diagram 3-16

In Diagram 3-16 we show the strongside defensive forward getting beaten to the basket after attempting to intercept a pass. The center drops back to stop the easy lay-up. Our strongside guard will leave his man and attempt to either cut the driving forward or help defend the pivot area. If the guard can stop the penetration, he does. The weakside guard moves down the lane and helps defend the pivot area and the basket. The weakside forward moves over to help defend the basket. The "beaten" strongside defensive forward must make a recovery to his own man or simply move towards the basket and pick up an open offensive player. In this case it may be the offensive center or strongside guard.

We have some basic rules that help in covering up the open man.

1. Our guards should never be split by a dribbler.
2. The guard and forward should never be split by a dribbler.
3. The center and forward should never be split by a dribbler.
4. The offensive player should be denied the cut to the ball.
5. No offensive player should be given the baseline drive.

These five rules not only help prevent us from having to cover up, but they also aid us in each player's understanding of when he should leave his man to help defend the basket. For example, assume that the driving guard gets away from his defender. The weakside guard immediately drops towards the basket into the foul line area to stop the penetration. The forwards drop toward the lane and basket. The center floats towards the basket in order to keep the action in front of him. The beaten defender would attempt to recover to his own man or move to take on the weakside defensive guard, depending on the situation. This action is shown in Diagram 3-17.

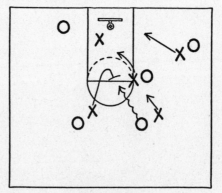

Diagram 3-17

What happens if the center is beaten by his man on the drive?

Our forwards immediately drop to defend the basket in order to prevent the easy lay-up and to prevent their men from sliding behind them for an easy shot. Our guards drop into the lane towards the basket, and the defensive center attempts to recover, as shown in Diagram 3-18.

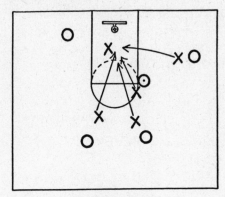

Diagram 3-18

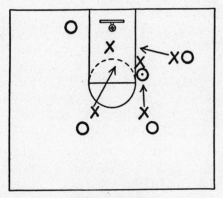

Diagram 3-19

It is our hope that one of the defensive guards will be in a position to stop the center's penetration before one of the defensive forwards is forced to pick up this driver. If the weakside forward is forced to commit to this driver, the weakside guard continues to drop and cover the weakside offensive forward. The strongside forward, in some situations, may also move across the lane and cover the basket if the weakside forward commits to the dribbler. One rule that helps us in this situation is that our players are instructed to drop towards the lane a step and a half if the offensive center receives the ball. This helps jam up the lane and force the pass back to the perimeter. Once the ball has been returned outside, our players move back into their overplay-pressure man-man positions. Actually, whenever the ball is passed into the pivot area, regardless of who the receiver is, we try to give help. Diagram 3-19 shows the movement of the defensive collapse when the offensive center has the basketball.

REBOUNDING ASSIGNMENTS AND TECHNIQUES

We ask all of our players to screen their men away from the basket after every shot until they know where the ball will bound. Once they read the bound of the ball, they are instructed to pursue the basketball with the utmost intensity. We usually have our players reverse pivot out of their defensive stance. They pivot to the direction that will block the offensive man's path to the basket. They pivot into a parallel stance with their knees in the flexed position, weight evenly distributed on the feet, head and shoulders up, looking toward the basket, hands up near the sides of the head, elbows out, and the offensive player on their rump. The rebounder slides when necessary to keep the offensive man behind him. A slight amount of contact will probably be made. Once the defender knows where the ball is going to bound, he makes an all-out effort to secure it for his team.

Another technique that we use when making the pivot during the screen-out is the "step-in" movement. Instead of pivoting from our defensive stance, our first movement is a step between the offensive man's feet and then we make the pivot. This usually freezes the offensive player momentarily because he anticipates a contact that does not occur. The defender must be careful not to step too deeply between the offensive man's feet or he will cause a foul.

DOUBLE-UP ASSIGNMENTS

Sometimes if the offensive player gives up his dribble in any one of three areas we will double-team the ball. Basically, we will double-team at the baseline low post, at the baseline corner, and at the sidelines. Diagram 3-20 shows the baseline low-post double team.

As illustrated in Diagram 3-20, the offensive forward has driven the baseline, but the defender cuts him off at the low post. The offensive man is forced to suspend his dribble. Once this has occurred, the strongside guard may choose to trap him with the aid of the defensive strongside forward. The weakside guard moves over to play the obvious potential pass to the strongside guard. The center shuts off the passing lane to the pivot and the weakside forward favors the basket.

Diagram 3-21 shows the double team in the baseline corner. The assignments are the same.

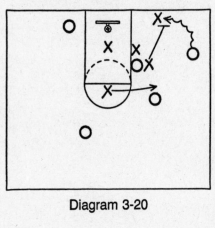

Diagram 3-20

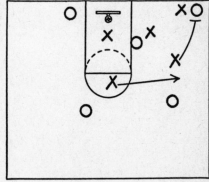

Diagram 3-21

Diagram 3-22 shows the guards double-teaming on the sideline. Once the offensive guard turns his back on the weak-side guard and begins dribbling out towards the side, this is the key for the double team. The weakside guard moves in for the trap and the weakside forward moves out to play the pass to the weakside guard.

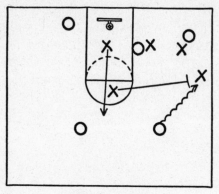

Diagram 3-22

COACHING AIDS

One coaching technique we've found to be extremely help-ful is for a coach to view part of his practices from the balcony. We usually have a coach in the balcony of our gym during most of our practice sessions. He has an excellent vantage point from there. He is able to see easily the weaknesses of our defense created by poor positioning and improper technique application.

Positioning is by far the most important ingredient in our defense. Looking at the defensive positioning from floor level, the coach will miss a great deal. For years, football coaches have had walkie-talkies in use from the press box by assistants. Basketball coaches should also use the same technique. The worst seat in the house is that one on the team bench. The coach simply can't see the floor from the proper perspective. We recommend that one of your assistants view practices and games from the balcony of your gym and relay information to you on the bench.

Another valuable coaching aid that we have used is game film. This is an excellent teaching aid to our team. We have

spliced together sequences of games to show the proper techniques that our players should use. Allowing players to see
themselves executing in a game situation is an excellent learning
opportunity for self-evaluation. It allows each player to learn
from his mistakes and improve his techniques.

4

Developing Individual Overplay-Pressure Defensive Skills

Drill is an extremely important part of a coach's repertoire. Time is a valuable commodity in practice and your utilization of proper defensive drills helps the players receive the maximum benefit from each practice session.

Before a practice drill can be considered useful, the participants must have a clear and total understanding of the expectations for each drill, the fundamental movements of the drill, and the reason for repeatedly executing the drill properly. If each player understands the importance of each activity or drill, he will be able to make his most intense effort. Intensity, both on a physical as well as a mental level, is vital to the improvement of the team; therefore, the coach must communicate his objectives to the players.

All defensive drills should be a simulation of those defensive situations that will occur during the actual contest. All practice situations should be as gamelike as possible. The players should be able to see this relationship. This will help promote player intensity in practice because they can see the need for each activity. Without player intensity in practice there will be very little improvement of the basketball skills necessary for success.

INNER DEFENSIVE DRILL

Rectangle 16-Foot Defender's Drill

The Rectangle 16-Foot Defender's Drill has been invaluable in helping to improve our team defense around the basket. Diagram 4-1 shows the basic alignment for this drill.

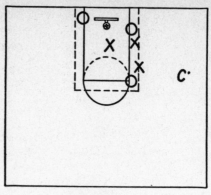

Diagram 4-1

Directions:

1. The players (three-on-three) must remain within a rectangle 16 feet in width and 16 feet in length.

2. The offensive players may set any screens they desire, or create any movement they deem necessary to free themselves for a pass from the coach (c).

3. The defenders overplay the passing lanes heavily and attempt to prevent the pass from being thrown into the offensive rectangle for a five-second count.

4. When the pass is completed before the five-second count expires, the players go three-on-three until the offense scores or the defense secures the rebound.

5. The coach throws the initial pass and should attempt to pass the ball inside the rectangle from both guard and forward positions.

6. The defenders should be able to learn when to front, how to overplay, what cuts to deny, how to favor the strong side, how to defend the backdoor lob, how to handle off the ball screens, and how to anticipate.

In Diagram 4-1 the defender at the high post is overplaying his man from the low-post side when the pass is entered from the strong side forward. The defender at the low post is fronting his man who is within ten feet of the basket. The weakside defensive forward is favoring the strong side and assuming an overplay position between his man and the basketball. He is positioned in the center of the court and is prepared to deny his man a cut towards the basket or a low-post cut to the strong side. He is also in a position to help defend the backdoor lob to the strongside offensive players. The strongside defenders are overplaying tenaciously, not allowing their men a cut to the ball, but allowing them to move to the weak side. The defenders learn to anticipate the eventual cut of the offensive men towards the basketball and the strong side.

If the pass is completed within five seconds, a game of three-on-three ensues. If the defenders prevent the offensive team from scoring for two consecutive times, a new defensive unit replaces them.

Fouls are not called, but the coach should not allow the players to use their hands illegally. The defenders should quickly learn how to position their bodies on defense and how to screen the offensive player away from the basket on a field goal attempt.

We have found that this drill increases the effectiveness of our inner defense. We usually spend 15 to 20 minutes on this drill each day if we have been getting exploited by the opponent's inside game. All of our players participate in this drill. Our guards benefit from this drill as much as the forwards and centers.

REACTION DRILLS

Shuffle Drill

One drill that we employ to improve a player's reaction to the basketball and to the man is the Shuffle Drill. Diagram 4-2 shows how we align the players for this drill.

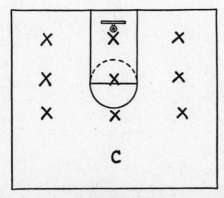

Diagram 4-2

Directions:

1. The players are aligned facing the coach and at least two arm lengths apart.
2. The players begin in a parallel stance.
3. The coach, via hand directions, has the players shuffle sideways in the parallel stance, backward left and right in the straddle stance, and forward left and right in the straddle.
4. The coach shall force the players to change directions quickly, allowing no round-house shuffles. The players must keep pace with the hand signal and make sharp angle moves when changing directions.
5. The coach should slowly increase the amount of time spent shuffling to build up the player's endurance in maintaining an aggressive defensive posture.

Defense is like dancing; the individual player must learn the fundamental steps used in good defensive shuffling. Once he learns the steps, his goal is to be able to move his feet as quickly as possible in order to successively react to the offensive player and the basketball.

The Shuffle Drill teaches the player the need to

- Keep one hand positioned to defend the shot.
- Keep one hand positioned to defend the dribble.
- Keep the feet shuffling on the floor.
- Keep the body balanced with the weight evenly distributed throughout the feet.
- Keep the knees flexed, body slightly bent at waist, and head up.
- Keep eyes on the ball handler's waist.

X-Ray Drill

A second drill used to improve the player's ability to react is the X-Ray Drill which was made popular by a great collegiate coach, John McLendon. Diagram 4-3 shows the alignment of this drill.

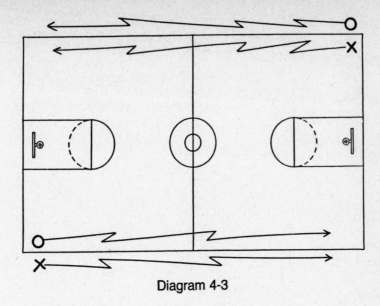

Diagram 4-3

Directions for execution of the X-Ray Drill:

1. The players divide themselves into pairs.
2. One player assumes the offensive role and works down the outside of the court using reverse movements.
3. The other player assumes the defensive role and guards the offensive player.
4. Once they reach the end of the court, they walk to the other side of the floor, reverse roles, and begin the drill again.
5. The defensive player must keep his eyes glued to the waist of the offensive player.

Three-Man Held Ball Drill

The Three-Man Held Ball Drill is another drill that helps improve the player's reaction ability. The drill is illustrated in Diagram 4-4.

Directions for the Three-Man Held Ball Drill:

1. The players are paired according to height and jumping ability.

2. Two players line up against each other while the third player tosses the ball into the air to create the jump ball situation.

3. The players rotate between all three positions.

This drill should help the players react to the throw of the ball, the height of the throw, the quickness of the release, and the jump of the opposing player.

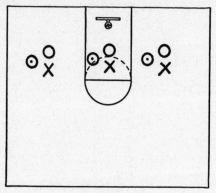

Diagram 4-4

LOOSE BALL DRILLS

Floor Burn Drill

There are two drills that we employ to help teach reaction to the loose ball. Diagram 4-5 illustrates our alignment for the Floor Burn Drill.

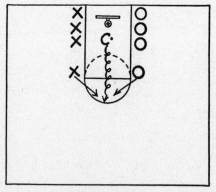

Diagram 4-5

Directions for the Floor Burn Drill:

1. The players form two lines at the mid-post area parallel to one another.

2. The coach has the basketball.

3. The coach rolls the ball toward the foul line.

4. The first player in each line will await a signal from the coach and thus pursue the basketball.

5. The player who recovers the loose ball becomes the offense and the other becomes the defense.

6. The offensive player will then drive to the far basket, playing one-on-one versus the defensive man.

The drill described in Diagram 4-5 is excellent for teaching players to go for the loose ball. It helps them overcome a fear of physical contact with the floor and other players. Once the players are on the floor grappling for the basketball, the drill teaches them to get to their feet immediately and play offense or defense, depending on who gained possession of the ball. This drill should help the players understand the importance of intensity and the value of a "never say die" attitude.

When the offensive player begins his drive downcourt to the far basket, the defender must learn how to slow the dribbler by getting ahead and gaining the guarding position. The offensive player will learn the value of driving downcourt quickly and "filling the gap" by keeping the defender on his backside as shown in Diagram 4-6.

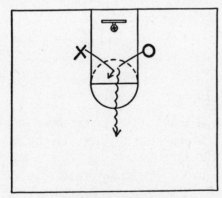

Diagram 4-6

Haul and Go Drill

Another fine loose ball drill is the Haul and Go. Diagram 4-7 illustrates the alignment for this drill.

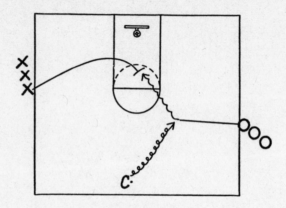

Diagram 4-7

Directions for the execution of the Haul and Go Drill:

1. The coach has the basketball at center court.
2. An offensive line forms at the hash mark on the center side of the court.
3. A defensive line forms opposite the foul line on the other side of the court.
4. The drill begins when the coach rolls the ball onto the playing floor and then signals the players to begin.
5. The first offensive player charges the ball, gains possession, and drives for the basket.
6. Once the offensive player touches the basketball, the defender protects the basket.

This drill teaches the offensive player to pick up the free basketball on the move and continue to drive toward the basket. The defensive player learns to cut off the driver in the open court. The defensive man should learn that his main job is to defend the basket from the drive if he doesn't secure the loose ball.

DENIAL DRILLS

Forward Denial Drill

Diagram 4-8 shows the alignment for the Forward Denial Drill.

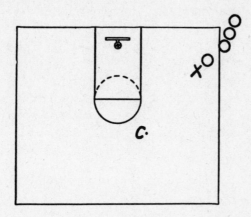

Diagram 4-8

Directions for the Forward Denial Drill:

1. The coach is the passer.
2. The players form a line at the corner of the floor.
3. The players rotate from offense to defense to the end of the line.
4. The coach signals play to begin by slapping the basketball.
5. The defensive player assumes the overplay denial position and attempts to prevent the offensive man from receiving a pass for five seconds.
6. If the offensive man receives the ball, he goes one-on-one with the defender until he scores or the defender gains control of the ball.

The defensive forward assumes the overplay position against the receiver. His ultimate goal is to prevent his man from receiving the basketball. He must always maintain the proper overplay position no matter how his man moves. Once the offensive forward receives the basketball, the defender hustles to the opposite side of his man and denies the dribbler the baseline penetration. The defender always gets away quickly to this side because in 90 percent of these situations the ball handler will drive away from the side just overplayed. Once the defender has recovered to the weak side, he plays one-on-one against the dribbler. He will attempt to turn the dribbler in the hope of forcing him to give up the dribble. When the shot is being taken, the defender attempts to change the shooter's arch, box the shooter from the rebound, and then pursue the basketball. This drill teaches many important fundamentals of the denial concept.

The player learns to:

1. Overplay
2. Deny the cut to the ball
3. Defend the backdoor cut
4. Maintain the proper guarding distance and form
5. Recover to the basket when out of position
6. Turn the dribbler
7. Deny the shot
8. Box-out
9. Pursue the rebound

Another area that deserves special mention is the technique of beating the offensive man to the spot. The player will learn to defend the areas ahead of the offensive man rather than ride skintight to the offensive man. In the overplay position he will learn to stay an arm's length away from the receiver and in the passing lane with his hand and arm as shown in Diagram 4-8. He learns to keep a three-foot gap between himself and the offensive receiver at all times. This forces the receiver to use two and a half steps to get open and allows the defender time to adjust to this movement.

Once the offensive man receives the pass, the defender will learn to give ground and beat the dribbler to an estimated spot on the floor, forcing a change of direction dribble.

Guard Denial Drill

Diagram 4-9 shows the alignment for the Guard Denial Drill. The objectives are exactly the same as in the Forward Denial Drill. Diagram 4-10 shows the Guard Denial Drill being practiced with the pass being thrown from the forward position.

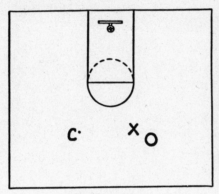
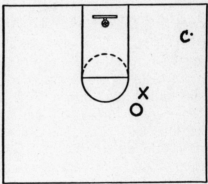

Diagram 4-9   Diagram 4-10

Post Denial Drill

Diagram 4-11 shows the Post Denial Drill.

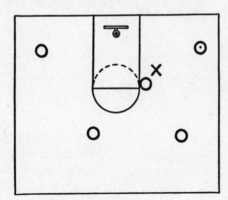

Diagram 4-11

Directions for the Post Denial Drill:

1. The basketball is moved from the guard and forward positions in a random manner.

2. The defensive center adjusts his position against the offensive center, depending on the position of the ball and man.

3. Once the basketball is received by the offensive center, a one-on-one game takes place.

4. Once the offensive center shoots the basketball, the defender boxes-out and then pursues the ball.

This is an excellent drill to help teach the defensive center the proper positioning techniques needed to defend the pivot area. The defensive center learns how to overplay, how to switch sides on his man, how to front, how to jam the strong side, and how to deny the strongside cut. Diagram 4-11 shows the four positions from which the basketball will be moved to create these different situations. The coach can instruct the offensive center and the passers to execute certain maneuvers to help isolate particular defensive situations for extra emphasis.

RECOVERY DRILLS

Two-Man Step-Away Drill

Diagrams 4-12 and 4-13 show the alignment for the Two-Man Step-Away Drill.

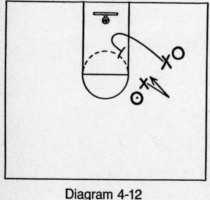

Diagram 4-12

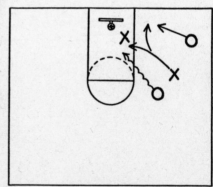

Diagram 4-13

Directions for executing the Two-Man Step-Away Drill:

1. The defensive guard takes one full step past the ball-handling guard.
2. When the defensive man steps past, the ball handler drives to the basket.
3. The second defensive man drops back to defend the basket, attempting to slow down the penetration until the beaten defender can recover to help.

Three-Man Step-Away Drill

Diagram 4-14 shows the Three-Man Step-Away Drill.

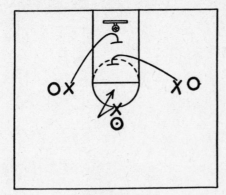

Diagram 4-14

Diagram 4-14 is the same drill as shown in Diagram 4-12. The only difference between these drills is that more men are involved. In Diagram 4-14 the middle man is practicing the recovery technique. The recovery move should also be practiced from the wing positions.

These recovery drills help teach the defenders the importance of making a second and third effort. To be an outstanding defensive player, the defender must never stop hustling. Hustling is another term for recovering from an error. Basketball is a game of errors and players must never pout about their mistakes. A good player learns from his mistakes but does not allow them to disrupt his effort.

FLOOR ANGLE DRILLS

Forward Angle Drill

Diagram 4-15 shows the formation for the Forward Angle Drill.

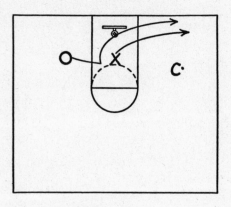

Diagram 4-15

Directions for executing the Forward Angle Drill:

1. The coach positions himself at a forward or guard spot and attempts to pass to the weakside forward cutting towards the basketball.
2. The defensive forward positions himself in the center of the lane directly between the ball and his man, taking away the opponent's direct angle cut to the ball.
3. The offensive forward will attempt to go directly to the ball; if denied, he will backdoor cut to the baseline.
4. The defender denies the high or direct cut, forces the offensive man to backdoor cut and beats him to the low post as shown in Diagram 4-16.

This drill teaches the defender to favor the strong side of the floor at all times. He learns to deny the obvious cut toward the basketball and mentally anticipates the backdoor cut to the baseline low post. In his mind he can see what angle he must use to beat his man to the baseline.

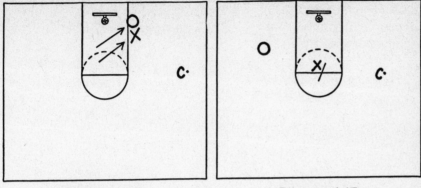

Diagram 4-16   Diagram 4-17

Diagram 4-17 shows the Forward Angle Drill being practiced with the addition of a stationary screen in the lane. The defender must learn to avoid the screen and still execute his defensive assignment.

Strongside Guard Angle Drill

Diagram 4-18 shows the alignment for the Strongside Guard Angle Drill.

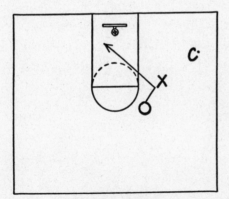

Diagram 4-18

Directions for the Strongside Guard Angle Drill:

1. The guard passes the basketball to the coach at the strongside forward position.
2. The offensive guard attempts to cut between the defensive guard and the ball. The defender prevents this cut by moving to the outside and denying the cut.

3. The defender lets the offensive guard go to the weak side. He remains between the offensive guard and ball in the center of the lane, waiting for the eventual return cut to the strong side. Diagram 4-19 shows this positioning. Diagram 4-20 shows the defender fronting the offensive guard if he cuts to the low post.

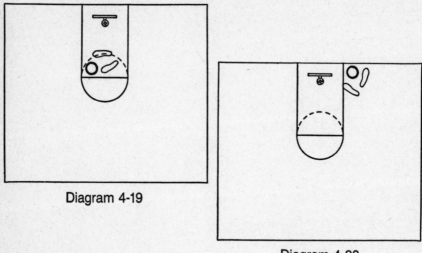

Diagram 4-19

Diagram 4-20

Weakside Guard Angle Drill

Diagram 4-21 shows the alignment for the Weakside Guard Angle Drill.

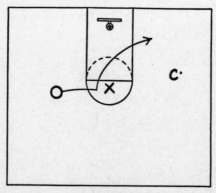

Diagram 4-21

Directions for the Weakside Guard Angle Drill:

1. The coach will attempt to pass the basketball to the weakside guard on a direct angle cut or a backdoor angle cut to the strongside low post.

2. The defender aligns himself favoring the strong side of the court and denies the offensive guard the direct angle cut to the basketball.

3. The offensive guard attempts to make the direct angle cut and then backdoors to the low post and baseline.

4. The defensive guard anticipates the backdoor cut and takes a direct angle cut to the baseline, beating his man to the strongside low post.

Turning the Dribbler Drill

Diagram 4-22 shows the alignment for the Turning the Dribbler Drill.

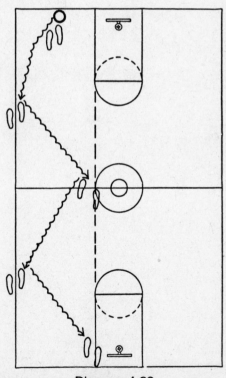

Diagram 4-22

Directions for Turning the Dribbler Drill:

1. Two parallel lines 20 feet apart running the length of the court should be marked.

2. The offensive player begins the drill by dribbling in a zig-zag pattern between the lines to the opposite end of the court.

3. The defender uses the straddle stance positioned a half-body to the outside of the dribbler. He maintains this overplay position forcing the dribbler to change directions as they advance downcourt.

4. When the dribbler changes direction, the defender takes two running steps and regains his overplay shuffle position.

This drill is invaluable because it teaches the defender how to pressure the dribbler without fouling or getting beaten by the drive.

PIVOT MAN DRILLS

One-on-One Pivot Drill

Diagram 4-23 shows the alignment for the One-on-One Pivot Drill.

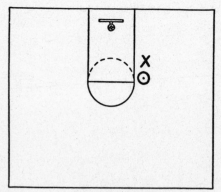

Diagram 4-23

Directions for the One-on-One Pivot Drill:

1. The offensive center assumes a high-post position with his back to the basket, holding the ball.

2. The offensive center has three seconds in which to attack the basket.

3. A game of one-on-one takes place until the defense gains control of the basketball or the offense scores. If the offensive player scores, he remains on offense.

The One-on-One Pivot Drill is a good power drill. The offensive post player should take the ball to the basket with authority. The defender must force the offensive man to go to his weakness and away from his strength. The defender should position a half-body to the outside, forcing the ball-handler to reverse dribble. The defender should always box-out when the shot is taken and then pursue the rebound.

Low-Post Front Drill

Diagram 4-24 shows the alignment for learning to front the low-post player. This is our Low-Post Front Drill.

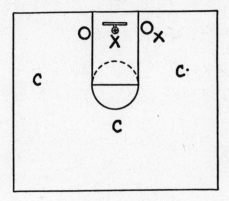

Diagram 4-24

Directions for the Low-Post Front Drill:

1. Three coaches assume the passing positions as shown in Diagram 4-24.

2. The ball should be moved at random among the three passers until it is passed inside.

3. When the basketball is on the side of the court, the strongside defender fronts, and the weakside defender favors the strong side, helping defend the backdoor lob.

In this drill the players learn how and when to front and how to defend the backdoor lob pass. This is an excellent drill to help strengthen the inner defense.

REBOUNDING DRILLS

Circle Box-Out Drill

Diagram 4-25 shows the alignment for the Circle Box-Out Drill.

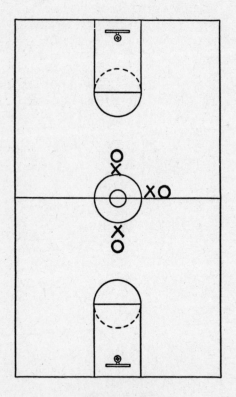

Diagram 4-25

Directions for the Circle Box-Out Drill:

1. Three pairs of offensive and defensive players gather around the jump ball circle.

2. The ball is placed on the floor in the center of the circle.

3. The coach blows the whistle to start the drill.

4. The defenders box-out the offensive players for three seconds.

This drill allows each defender to work on his pivot and box-out maneuver without concerning himself with ball pursuit.

Two-on-Two Rebounding Drill

Diagram 4-26 shows the formation for the Two-on-Two Rebounding Drill.

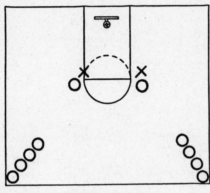

Diagram 4-26

Directions for the Two-on-Two Rebounding Drill:

1. Two lines are formed. The players rotate from receivers, to offensive rebounders, to defensive rebounders, to the receivers.

2. The coach begins the drill by shooting the basketball.

3. The defensive rebounders box-out and then pursue the basketball.

4. Once the defensive rebounder gains control of the ball, he makes an exit pass to either receiver at the exit area.

This is a fine rebounding drill because all the proper rebounding techniques are taught. Especially important is the development of the exit pass after the rebound is secured. We usually make the defensive rebounders execute this drill until every fundamental is correctly completed.

Pursuit Rebounding Drill

Diagram 4-27 shows the alignment for the Pursuit Rebounding Drill.

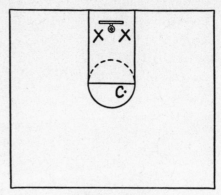

Diagram 4-27

Directions for the Pursuit Rebounding Drill:

1. A shooting ring should be placed inside the rim of the basket.
2. Two players line up near the basket.
3. No fouls are called unless they are intentional or malicious.
4. The coach shoots the basketball.
5. The two players pursue the rebound.
6. The first player to rebound the ball and score wins the game.

This is an outstanding drill to get the rebounders playing aggressively. If the coach has no ring for the basket, a game of three baskets would serve the same purpose.

WEAVE DRILLS

Screen Free Weave Drill

One of the coaches in our conference always seems to run the figure eight weave pattern offense. This can be very effective if the defenders are not schooled in the art of avoiding the block that results on the handoff.

Diagram 4-28 shows the alignment for the Screen Free Weave Drill.

Directions for the Screen Free Weave Drill.

1. The defenders practice shuffling behind the handoff block and also sliding over the top, preventing the hand-off from taking place.

2. The offensive players form or execute the figure eight pattern.

Diagram 4-29 shows the defender shuffling to the inside of the handoff. (No switches occur.)

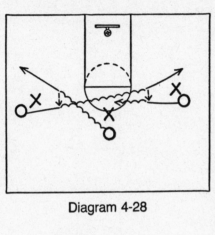

Diagram 4-28

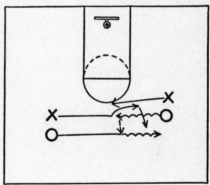

Diagram 4-29

High-Post Screen Weave Drill

After the defenders have practiced the Weave Drill, we add a screener to the drill. We then practice the High-Post Screen Weave Drill, Diagram 4-30.

The defender will practice fighting over and sliding behind this high-post screen. This drill teaches the defender how to shuffle, anticipate screens, and how to remain no more than one man removed from the ball handler at any time.

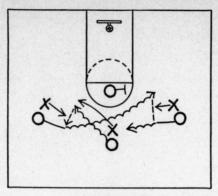

Diagram 4-30

SCISSOR DRILLS

Guard Split Post Drill

Diagram 4-31 shows the alignment for the Guard Split Post Drill.

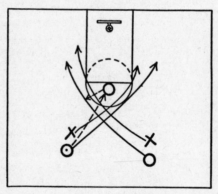

Diagram 4-31

Directions for the Guard Split Post Drill:

1. A pivot player positions himself at the high post. Two guards position themselves at normal guard areas.

2. Offensive guard #1 makes the pass to the pivot and cuts over the top. Offensive guard #2 cuts over the pivot and off of the heels of guard #1.

3. We teach two options:
   a. Both defensive guards stay a half-body ahead of the cutter and go over the pivot with him as shown in Diagram 4-31.

b. The defensive guards switch men while the split is being made as shown in Diagram 4-33.

4. The defensive guards are to deny their men the basketball.

Pivot Split Pick-Up Drill

Diagrams 4-32A and 4-32B show the alignment for the Pivot Split Pick-Up Drill.

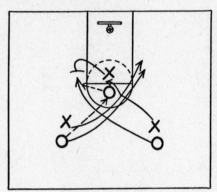

Diagram 4-32A   Diagram 4-32B

Directions for the Pivot Split Pick-Up Drill:

1. The alignment is basically the same as in the Guard Split Post Drill, the only difference being the addition of a defensive center.

2. The defensive center calls out, "Split" to let the defensive guards know the split post play is coming.

3. On hearing the center call the split, the two guards jump back on even line with the defensive center.

4. The two defensive guards wait to pick up the cutting guards as they go around the screen.

   The beaten guard must either:

   a. Recover to the basket and defend the offensive center.

   b. Recover to his own man by sliding behind the offensive pivot and to the driver, allowing the defensive center to return to the offensive center.

5. The defensive center must learn that he is responsible for defending the basket against this type of penetration. The

defensive center must be basket-conscious and yet maintain responsibility for the offensive center.

The split post drills that we have discussed are excellent for teaching the players to anticipate offensive movement. These drills stress the importance of determination, hustle, and recovery.

PASSING GAME DRILLS

Four-Man Double Down Drill

Diagrams 4-33, 4-34, 4-35, and 4-36 show the alignment of the Four-Man Double Down Drill.

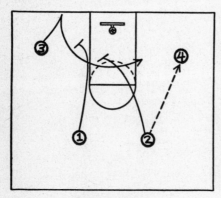

Diagram 4-33

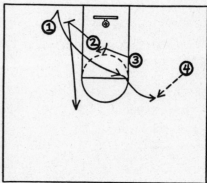

Diagram 4-34

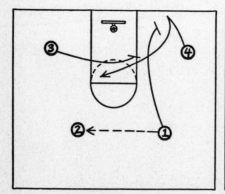

Diagram 4-35

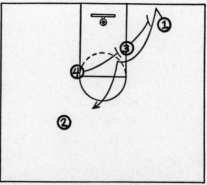

Diagram 4-36

Directions for the Four-Man Double Down Drill:

1. The offensive team executes the basic screen away, base-line touch, and return ball movement of the passing game offense.

2. We usually begin execution of the drill by disallowing the dribble by the offense.

3. The defenders learn to fight over the screens, jam the strong side, beat their man to the spot, use the angles of the floor, deny their man the ball, and other principles of the overplay defense.

4. The dribble may be added to the drill at the coach's descretion. This will change the complexion of the drill and involve more principles of the overplay defense.

Three-Man Movement Drill

Another passing game offense drill is the Three-Man Movement Drill. Diagram 4-37 shows the alignment for this drill.

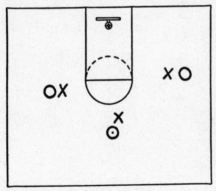

Diagram 4-37

Directions for the Three-Man Movement Drill:

1. The point has the ball to begin the drill.

2. Basically, the offensive players have the following options:

   a. Screen for a man who does not have the basketball.

   b. Cut to the basket and away from the basketball.

   c. Never stand for more than three seconds.

d. Screen for the man with the basketball.

e. Drive the basket when possible.

3. The coach may limit the number of options as needed.

4. The coach may or may not allow the offensive team to dribble.

5. The defense will be working hard to deny the receivers the basketball and applying all the other man-man overplay fundamentals.

The passing game drills are outstanding because they require the employment of all the fundamentals that the defensive players will need in actual game situations.

SCREEN-AND-ROLL DRILLS

Over-Under Drill

Diagrams 4-38 and 4-39 show the alignment for the Over-Under Drill.

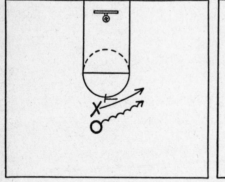 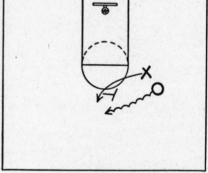

| Diagram 4-38 | Diagram 4-39 |

Directions for the Over-Under Drill:

1. In this drill there is a single stationary screen.

2. The dribbler goes over the screen twice, once from the left and once from the right.

3. The defender must stay a half-body ahead of the dribbler and slide over the screen.

4. When the dribbler reverses direction, the defender will slide behind the screen and quickly return to the dribbler.

Two-on-Two Screen Drill

Diagrams 4-40 and 4-41 show the alignment for the Two-on-Two Drill.

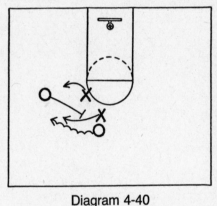

Diagram 4-40

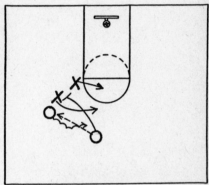

Diagram 4-41

Directions for executing the Two-on-Two Screen Drill:

1. Diagram 4-40 shows the forward screening for the guard. Diagram 4-41 shows the guard screening for the forward. Both types of screening situations may be utilized in practice.

2. In Diagram 4-40 the defensive forward calls out the position of the screener to the defensive guard.

3. The forward steps away from the screener to allow the defensive guard the opportunity to slide behind the screen if necessary. The defensive forward shifts to the outside of the screener as he steps away in order to help protect against the dribbler coming off the screen and going to the basket as portrayed in Diagram 4-41.

Double Screen Drill

Diagram 4-42 shows the alignment of the Double Screen Drill.

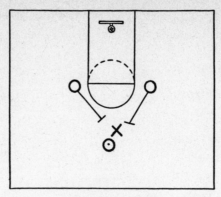

Diagram 4-42

Directions for executing the Double Screen Drill:

1. Two stationary screens are aligned at the side of the key.
2. The dribbler mentally determines which screen to use.
3. The defender attempts to fight over the screen.

These screen-and-roll drills teach the players how to anticipate screens, the importance of talking on defense, and how to fight over screens. The players also learn how to give help without giving up their own men.

COVER-UP DRILLS

Full-Court Dribble Cut-Off Drill

Diagram 4-43 shows the alignment for the Full-Court Dribble Cut-Off Drill.

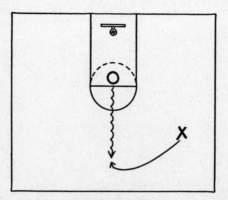

Diagram 4-43

Directions for the Full-Court Dribble Cut-Off Drill:

1. The dribbler begins his drive for the basket on the first whistle.

2. The defender is placed at the hash mark. On the second whistle, the defender goes downcourt and attempts to defend the dribbler.

This is an excellent drill for teaching players using the press to stay below the level of the basketball. It also teaches the defenders to deny penetration downcourt by an uncontested dribbler.

3-2 2-1 Drill

Diagrams 4-44, 4-45, and 4-46 show the alignment for our 3-2 2-1 Drill.

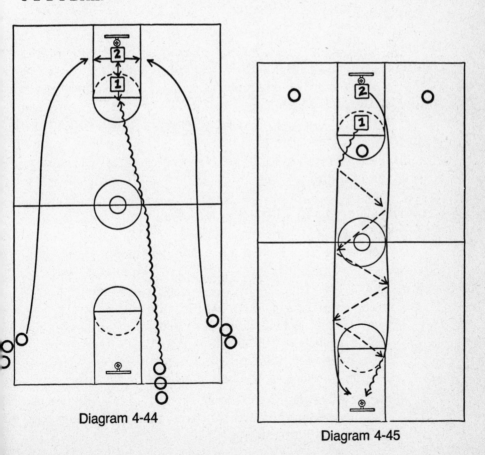

Diagram 4-44

Diagram 4-45

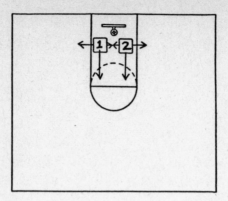

Diagram 4-46

Directions for executing the 3-2 2-1 Drill:

1. Three lines are formed at the end of the court.

2. Two defenders are set in tandem at the opposite basket.

3. The first man in each line advances downcourt, keeping the ball in the center of the floor.

4. Player #1 in the tandem stops the penetration of the middle man at the foul line. If the basketball is passed to a wing man by the middle man, #1 will move to the basket, keeping his head on the basketball and preventing the ball from being passed from wing to wing across the lane.

5. Player #2 moves to the wing man, preventing the drive to the baseline.

6. Once the play is over, the two defensive players go on offense against the lone middle man who now assumes a defensive role for the opposite basket, as shown in Diagram 4-45. The two wing men become the new defensive tandem.

7. In the 2-1 situation, the one defender hustles back to protect the basket and positions himself to guard both men. He attempts, through his positioning and defensive faking, to get the dribbler to pick up the ball prematurely, to draw a charging foul, or to encourage the offensive players to overpass the ball, thus creating a turnover.

8. In the 3-2 situation (illustrated in Diagram 4-46), we also have the defenders work out of a lateral arrangement instead of a tandem.

The 3-2 2-1 Drill is a fantastic drill to help build aggressive defenders. In the 3-2 situation the defenders learn to rely on each other and to quickly cover up for one another. They learn quickly how to protect the basket. Their rebounding skills also develop. The defenders rapidly learn the value of intensive ball pursuit in rebounding.

In the 2-1 phase the defender learns to get back to the basket and not get beaten in the open court. He learns how to fake defensive maneuvers in order to slow down the offensive players, confuse them and force an error. He learns that one man can beat two men on occasion.

This is also an outstanding drill for the development of correct passing techniques by the offensive players. It also helps players learn the basic lanes of the fast-break offense.

OVERPLAY DRILL

One-on-One Ball Drill

Diagram 4-47 shows the alignment of our One-on-One Ball Drill.

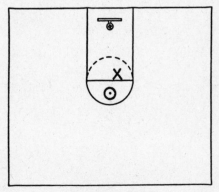

Diagram 4-47

Directions for the One-on-One Ball Drill:

1. The offensive player prepares to accept the basketball from the defender to begin the drill at the foul line.

2. The defender assumes his straddle stance position a half-body to the outside of the offensive man's dominant side. If the offensive player is right-handed, the defender is

overplaying to that side. When he is prepared, the defender hands the basketball to the offensive player.

3. Once the offensive player has the ball, he should attack the basket within three seconds.

4. The defender is barely more than an arm's length from the offensive player, attempting to deny him the shot or the drive.

5. The defender is ready to give ground in order to turn the direction of the dribbler.

6. Once the shot is about to be taken, the defender uses his hand to force a change of arc and screens the offensive man from the basket.

7. We play make it, take it.

The One-on-One Ball Drill is invaluable in developing a defender who will attack the man handling the basketball. It teaches him to defend the basket and halt the dribbler. He learns to contest every movement by the offensive man and to limit the offensive man's options.

SKILLS TAUGHT ON EACH LEVEL

We attempt to put special emphasis on certain skills at each competitive level.

Skills of special emphasis at the ninth grade level:

a. Forward Denial Drill

b. Guard Denial Drill

c. Post Denial Drill

d. One-on-One Ball Drill

e. Shuffle Drill

f. Turning the Dribbler Drill

g. Two-on-Two Rebounding Drill

h. Over-Under Drill

i. 3-2 2-1 Drill

Skills of special emphasis at the tenth grade level:

a. All skills taught on the freshmen level are continually refined on this level.

b. Special attention on Denial Drills

c. Forward Angle Drill

d. Strongside Guard Angle Drill

e. Weakside Guard Angle Drill

f. Floor Burn Drill

g. Two-Man Step-Away Drill

h. Low-Post Front Drill

i. Guard Split Post Drill

j. Two-on-Two Screen Drill

k. Circle Box Drill

Skills of special emphasis at the eleventh and twelfth grade levels:

a. Constant review of drills taught on previous levels.

b. Special review of all Denial and Floor Angle Drills.

c. Rectangle 16-Foot Defender's Drill

d. Haul and Go Drill

e. Three-Man Step-Away Drill

f. Pursuit Rebounding Drill

g. Four-Man Double Down Drill

h. Three-Man Movement Drill

i. Double Screen Drill

On the varsity level we are constantly practicing the Denial and Floor Angle Drills. These are the bases for our entire defense. The varsity coaches also must strengthen all skill areas that are not properly developed.

The drills listed for the various levels are not the only drills used at those levels. These are the drills we feel must be presented to build a strong defense in time for the player's senior year. Each coach is still responsible for the needs of his players.

TYPICAL DEFENSIVE PRACTICE SCHEDULE
(WEEK)

Monday

    3:00-3:20 3-2 2-1 Drill
    3:20-3:40 One-on-One Ball Drill
    3:40-4:00 Forward Denial Drill and Guard Denial Drill
    4:00-4:20 Rectangle 16-Foot Defender's Drill

Tuesday

    3:00-3:20 3-2 2-1 Drill
    3:20-3:40 One-on-One Ball Drill
    3:40-4:00 Post Denial Drill
    3:40-4:00 Strongside Guard Angle Drill
    4:00-4:20 Forward Angle Drill
    4:00-4:20 Weakside Guard Angle Drill

Wednesday

    3:00-3:20 One-on-One Ball Drill
    3:20-3:30 Circle Box Drill
    3:30-3:50 Rectangle 16-Foot Defender's Drill
    3:50-4:00 Pursuit Rebounding Drill
    4:00-4:20 Three-Man Movement Drill

Thursday

    3:00-3:20 3-2 2-1 Drill
    3:20-3:40 Forward Denial Drill (Guards)
    3:20-3:40 Guard Denial Drill (Forwards)
    3:40-4:00 Forward Angle Drill (Guards)
    3:40-4:00 Weakside Guard Angle Drill (Forwards)
    4:00-4:15 Three-Man Step-Away Drill
    4:15-4:30 Double Screen Drill

Friday

> 3:00-3:20 One-on-One Ball Drill
>
> 3:20-3:35 Post Denial Drill
>
> 3:35-3:50 Low-Post Denial Drill
>
> 3:50-4:00 Pursuit Rebounding Drill
>
> 4:00-4:20 Four-Man Double Down Drill

In this simulated practice week schedule, we attempt to cover some of the most important basics of our defense. We also rotate our players through the drills in order to give each man experience at the different positions. The players should gain a better understanding of our overall defense and improve their individual defensive skills.

By reading our practice schedule carefully, one can see that great emphasis is placed on our One-on-One Ball Drill. We feel that this drill helps us improve our aggressiveness, defensive skills, and rebounding skills. We place great emphasis on dictating to the ball handler what we will allow him to do with the ball. We will try to limit his options and force him away from his strengths.

5

Changing Game Pace with the Overplay-Pressure Defense

SCOUTING KEYS

As discussed in Chapter 2, the scouting report is a crucial tool in learning as much as possible about the opponents before the contest. Attempting to change the pace of a game by using the defense is not an easy task. There will be some techniques a coach may try that will have no effect whatsoever on the opponent. Yet, other changes may have a devastating effect on altering the pace of the game and determining the outcome. We attempt to avoid needless defensive changes during the game by basing our decisions on the scouting report.

What should the scout and coach be looking for when collecting data on the opposition? Here are some key areas of concern:

1. Does one man attempt to handle the ball against the presses?

2. Are they able to get the ball on the floor easily against the presses?

3. Do quick double-teams on the inbounds pass prove disruptive to their offense?

4. Are delayed double-teams at different court levels effective?

5. How do they react to varying full-court defenses? (Example: man-man press with ball out-of-bounds to 1-2-1-1 press after the inbounds pass is completed and man-man at the half-court level.)

6. On which side of the midcourt line does pressure cause them the most trouble? (This refers to double-teams or straight man-man overplay.)

7. Rate each player's ball-handling ability.

8. What pass triggers their offensive movement? Can this pass be prevented?

9. Is this team predominantly working on the right or left side of the court?

10. As a team, where do the majority of shots occur?

11. Who are their main scoring threats?

12. Do they take the ball to the basket via the dribble or the pass?

13. How hard does each player work to free himself for a pass?

14. How far from the basket do the offensive players set up when executing their half-court offense?

15. How well do they react to varying pressure levels at the half-court area?

16. How well do they react to varying defensive types (1-2-2 zone, 1-3-1 trap, box and one, or man-man)?

17. What defense do other teams play against them and why?

18. What is their most glaring offensive weakness?

19. Where is the ball tipped during jump ball situations?

20. Do they signal where the ball will be tipped?

21. Do they run a play from a tipping situation?

22. Can we sneak an extra rebounder to the basket when shooting a free throw?

23. What major tendency do they have when executing out-of-bounds plays?

24. What predictable movement is executed on their fast break?

Ball Red

This may be a devastating defense at the half-court level. A half-court man-man press would closely describe this defense.

Diagram 5-1 shows the basic alignment of our defense as the basketball advances toward the midcourt line.

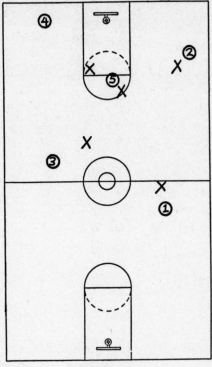

Diagram 5-1

As player #1 advances the basketball, the defender will begin his attack at the midcourt line. The defenders attempt to force this ball handler to pick up his dribble near the midcourt line. By forcing the dribbler to change directions several times quickly, and using hand fakes, this may be accomplished. Once this has been done, the defender moves in to the man and tries to deflect the pass.

As the dribbler was advancing the basketball in Diagram 5-1, the strongside forward and center were overplaying their man. The weakside guard and forward were favoring the strong side of the court. When the ball handler relinquishes his dribble, the weakside players aggressively overplay their men also. We now have one man fighting the pass and four men in a total overplay defense as shown in Diagram 5-2.

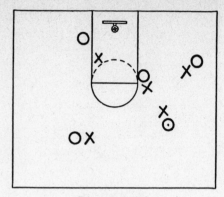

Diagram 5-2

Many times we won't be able to force the ball handler to pick up his dribble where and when we want. Therefore, we'll continue to play a conventional strongside overplay with weakside help until a situation arises where an offensive player picks up his dribble. At that moment the man guarding the ball handler may yell, "Ball!" We then go into the total overplay defense as shown in Diagram 5-3.

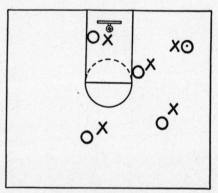

Diagram 5-3

This diagram shows the Ball Red being applied from the forward position.

In this defense we are going for the interception or the held ball situation. How successful will the opponents be in completing the backdoor pass against the overplay? If the defender guarding the passer does a good job of fighting the pass with his hands, the passer will have a tendency to throw a high arching pass to the backdoor cutter. Our defender guarding the backdoor cutter, as well as the weakside defenders, will have some success in intercepting this type of pass.

A coach can employ this defense for an entire game and keep a great deal of pressure on the offensive team. Another way to employ this defense is to use it periodically throughout the game. In some games it may be saved for crucial situations when a quick interception is needed. It has, for example, been quite successful against certain stalls.

One-Man Sag

Diagram 5-4 shows the alignment for the One-Man Sag.

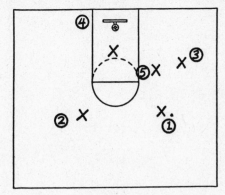

Diagram 5-4

The defender guarding the ball handler pressures him and attempts to make his advancement of the basketball difficult. The strongside forward, strongside guard, and center are in this overplay position. The man furthest from the basketball sags to the strong side favoring the ball.

This defense helps keep pressure on the basketball and on all receivers who are one direct pass from the basketball. It forces the offense to move hurriedly in order to execute any type of offensive pattern. This should help speed up the tempo and force the opponents to rush their shots.

This type of defensive alignment is vulnerable to the drive because of the great amount of pressure being placed in the passing lanes. However, if the defenders work diligently in practice on their defensive skills with emphasis on the floor angle, recovery, and cover-up drills, the danger of successful penetrations should be limited. It should be noted that the man sagging can greatly reduce the danger of a successful penetration by properly positioning himself between his man, the ball, and the basket.

Two-Man Sag

Diagram 5-5 shows the basic alignment of the Two-Man Sag.

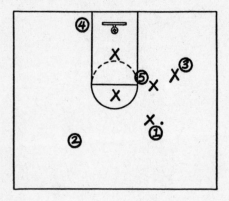

Diagram 5-5

The strongside defenders are in the overplay position with the weakside defenders shifting toward the strong side favoring the basketball. The weakside defenders attempt to shift towards the ball and to the center of the court. This type of set creates a great amount of pressure on the ball handler and the strongside receivers. It also results in a good weakside sag that helps defend against the drive, short jump shot, and backdoor pass. The weakside defenders are employing a sag that is similar to that seen in a 2-3 zone defense.

If the basketball is moved to the weak side, as drawn in Diagram 5-6, the defender simply exchanges roles.

What happens if the weakside offensive players move to the strong side?

In Diagram 5-5 the strongside guard has the basketball. Let's assume that players #2 and #4 cut to the strong side as shown in Diagram 5-7.

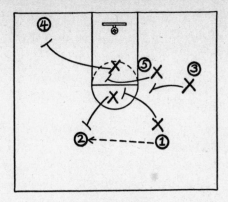

Diagram 5-6

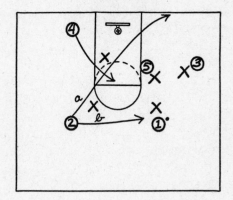

Diagram 5-7

As players #4 and #2 cross the parallel center of the court, the defenders assume their usual strongside overplay positions and deny their players the ball.

When playing the Two-Man Sag, we have three rules that govern the men playing the sag phase of the defense. They are:

1. When defending from the weak side of the court, sag towards the basketball.

2. When the receiver is two passes from the basketball, the defender should sag.

3. When defending on the weak side, the defenders should sag to the strong side between their men and the ball.

In Diagram 5-7 player #2 may make either cut "a" or "b." If he makes cut "a" to the baseline, the receiver is two passes from the basketball and the defender sags. If he makes cut "b" and goes toward the basketball, the defender would overplay and deny him the basketball.

FUNNELING OFFENSIVE PLAY

Another technique that we sometimes use is called funneling the basketball. There are different areas that we may choose to funnel or force the dribbler. Our favorite movement is to force the dribbler to the sideline. We overplay the strongside forward doggedly and at the same time, force the dribbler to the sideline. The defender overplays the dribbler to the inside, forcing him to the outside as shown in Diagram 5-8.

When the dribbler approaches the sideline with his back and head turned away from the weakside guard, we attempt double-team action on the dribbler. Diagram 5-9 shows the double-team maneuver of the defensive players involved.

In Diagram 5-9 the weakside guard moves in from the blindside and double-teams #1 with the strongside guard. Our strongside forward and center anticipate the pass to their men. The open man on the switch is #2. We cover #2, the weakside offensive guard, with our weakside forward who attempts to intercept the pass from #1 to #2. We double-team and play for the pass that #1 will attempt to throw from our double-team maneuver. If we miss the interception, our defenders return to their man-man defense.

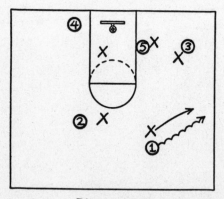

Diagram 5-8

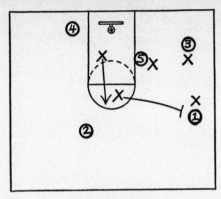

Diagram 5-9

This defense disrupts most offensive systems. We have had the most success by using this defense at key times during the game. Basically, it has been used as a surprise tactic to unsettle the offense with a quick interception.

Another technique of funneling would be to force the basketball to the foul line. Some years it has been our good fortune to have a big, shot-blocking center in the middle of our defense. When this talent lends itself to us, we may attempt to force the ball towards the middle when playing certain teams or in certain situations. Most of the time we are attempting to keep the ball from going to the middle because the offense has too many options from that area.

Diagram 5-10 shows our defender overplaying the ball handler to the outside and the alignment of our other players.

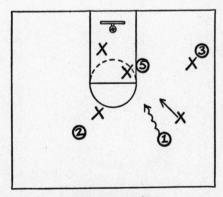

Diagram 5-10

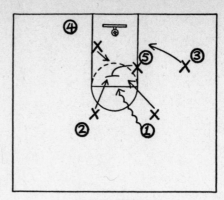

Diagram 5-11

Our defense is funneling the basketball to the middle from the Two-Man Sag. In this diagram the defensive guard is forcing the ball to the foul line while the weakside guard and forward play their normal sag positions to help strengthen our inner defense. The defensive center is ready to step to the basket and goal-tend the hoop if the dribbler gets too deep on his penetration as displayed in Diagram 5-11.

In Diagram 5-11 our defensive center drops to the inside and defends the basket. Our weakside forward and guard give help by going into the lane and jamming against the penetration. If the center can successfully goal-tend the basket, the other defenders can attempt to intercept the pass by #1.

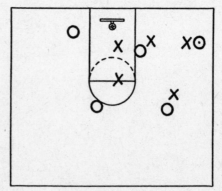

Diagram 5-12

Diagram 5-12 shows the same defense from the forward position.

Center Responsibility

We attempt to impress upon our defensive center the need to step towards the basket, keeping the driver in front of him. He should always expect weakside help from his teammates. Our defensive post player makes certain that the penetrator has to stop and shoot over him. He must always stay between the ball and the basket, keeping his man and the driver in front of him. He should always have the opportunity to:

a. block the shot

b. change the arch of the shot

The shot-blocking center should go for the ball after it leaves the shooter's hand. This should help him avoid the cheap foul on the shooter's arm or wrist. Another important factor when blocking a shot is to keep the ball in play. Slapping the intended shot into the stadium bleachers serves only to give the opposition the basketball once again. We want our center to deflect the shot to one of his teammates in order to initiate the fast break. On rare occasions we've had some gifted centers who could deflect the shot and catch the ball themselves. A gifted shot blocker can really make this defense devastating on the high school level.

BACKDOOR DOUBLE TEAMS

Diagram 5-13 shows the basketball being forced to the baseline.

The defensive forward forces his man toward the baseline and then attempts to cut him off at the low post. The strongside guard (X_1) leaves his man as soon as the ball handler turns his head on his drive to the baseline.

Diagram 5-14 shows the defensive shifts and movements of X_1 and X_3 as they double-team O_3.

In Diagram 5-14 the strongside forward has cut the dribbler at the baseline. The strongside guard has moved in for the double team. The weakside guard moves to player #1 and all defenders are looking for the first pass interception.

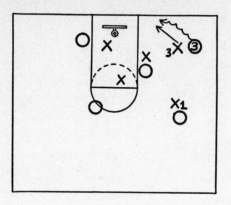

Diagram 5-13

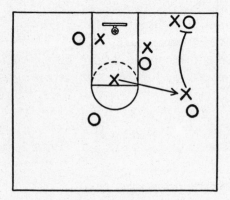

Diagram 5-14

Diagram 5-15 shows the shift of the defensive players in applying the backdoor double team against the pass from #1 to #3.

Diagram 5-16 shows the players positioning after the shift has been made.

This same diagram portrays the weakside forward double-teaming #3 with the strongside forward, F_3. Our weakside guard, G_2, moves back to play for the interception from #3 to #4. We attempt to intercept the pass that must be thrown from this double team. If we miss the interception, we return to our overplay positions.

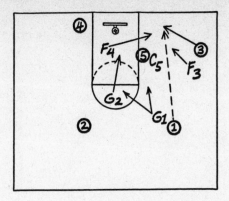

Diagram 5-15

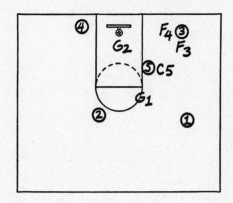

Diagram 5-16

Match-Up Traps

In order to execute our Match-Up Trap Defense, we align in our basic One-Man Sag as shown in Diagram 5-17.

Diagram 5-18 shows how we shift into our Match-Up Trap Defense.

The traps begin with the first pass. In Diagram 5-18, #1 passes to the strongside forward, #3. Our strongside guard, G_1, goes to the pass and traps with the strongside forward, F_3. The weakside defensive guard, G_2, moves across the court and becomes the point guard on defense. He helps discourage the pass to the pivot position. The weakside forward, F_4, remains at the low-post weak side for rebounding purposes. C_5, the defensive center, moves to the mid-post area to defend the basket.

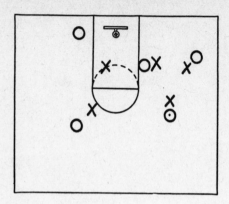

Diagram 5-17

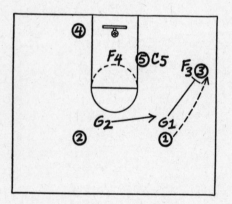

Diagram 5-18

Diagram 5-19 shows the shift if the pass is returned to #1, the strongside offensive guard.

As the ball is passed back to #1 from #3 in Diagram 5-19, G_2 traps with G_1. F_4 moves to help discourage the pass to the high post. F_3 moves toward the lane slightly, anticipating the pass to #3. C_5 shifts behind the high post, ready to defend the crosscourt pass.

To continue the sequence, Diagram 5-20 demonstrates the basketball being passed from #1 to #2 and the defensive shifts that result.

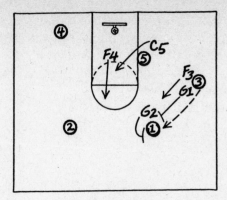

Diagram 5-19

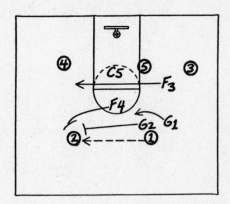

Diagram 5-20

In Diagram 5-20, F_4 traps between #2 and #4 to cause a lob over his hands. G_2 follows with the same positioning. F_3 crosses the court in front of C_5 and anticipates the pass to #4. C_5 shifts between the ball and the basket around the dotted line area in the lane with responsibility for the crosscourt pass to #3. G_1 moves to the middle to help discourage the high-post pass.

As continuation for this sequence, in Diagram 5-21, #2 passes to #4 and the defensive shifts are shown.

Diagram 5-21 indicates that F_3 traps #4 with F_4. G_2 defends the high post. G_1 rebounds the weak side; C_5 moves low to defend the basket.

If the initial pass would have been thrown from #4 to #2, the movements of the defenders would be reversed. F_4 would be responsible for the baseline traps. G_2 would be trapping on the wing. G_1 would be the point defender. F_3 would be trapping on the wing. C_5 remains with the same assignment.

We feel that this is a fine trapping defense if our center is an adept shot blocker. It allows us to keep him near the basket in a position to intimidate the short jump shooter.

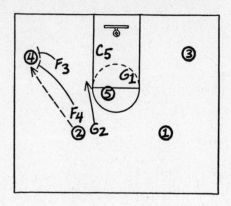

Diagram 5-21

If we do not have the big, shot-blocking center, we change our shifts accordingly. Diagram 5-22 shows the way we shift from our man-to-man when #2 passes to #4.

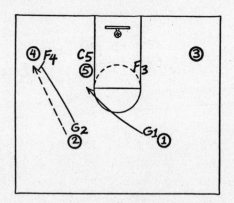

Diagram 5-22

The shifts in Diagram 5-22 are the same as in Diagram 5-18.

Diagram 5-23 shows how the shifts differ when #4 passes the ball back to #2.

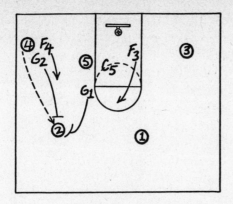

Diagram 5-23

G$_1$ in Diagram 5-23 becomes the point defender and traps #2 with G$_2$, who will assume a wing position. F$_4$ floats toward the lane anticipating the pass back to #4 and helping with the post area. F$_3$ moves forward to help discourage the pass to the high post. C$_5$ floats into the lane at the dotted line, helping with the high post and looking for the crosscourt pass.

Diagram 5-24 shows the defensive shift when #2 passes to #1. F$_3$ and G$_1$ trap #1. C$_5$ anticipates the pass to #4. F$_4$ plays the pass to #3. G$_2$ defends the pass to the high post.

Diagram 5-25 shows the completed shift when #1 passes to #3.

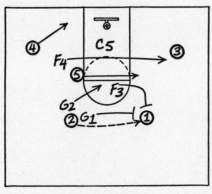

Diagram 5-24

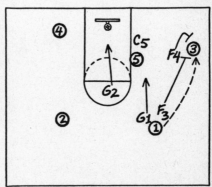

Diagram 5-25

Diagram 5-26 demonstrates our defensive shift if the first offensive pass is from guard to guard or if our weakside guard decides to initiate the defense by trapping the dribbling strong-side guard in the coffin corner.

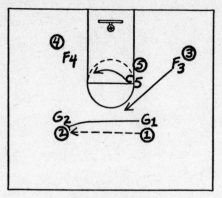

Diagram 5-26

OUT-OF-BOUNDS ADJUSTMENTS

Diagram 5-27 and 5-28 show some man-man defensive alignments on out-of-bounds situations.

In both diagrams our defense plays man-man against the offense. Diagram 5-27 shows a Two-Man Sag with the man playing the ball or passer helping to jam the basket. This helps

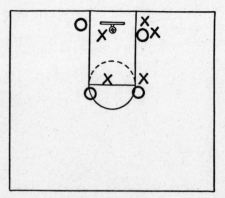

Diagram 5-27

prevent the easy lay-up on the inbounds pass. Diagram 5-28 shows X_3 defending the thrower, playing a floater position, discouraging the inbounds pass to the middle of the defense.

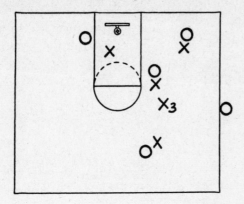

Diagram 5-28

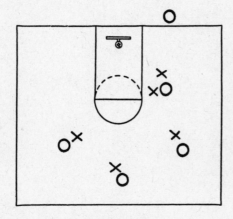

Diagram 5-29

Diagram 5-29 shows the inbounds double team on the opponent's best ball handler at the full-court level. We are trying to force one of the opponent's poorer ball handlers to take the inbounds pass. The percentages favor the turnover if this can be accomplished.

FREE THROW DEFENSIVE PLAY

In Diagram 5-30 the defensive team is aligned for the free throw by the opponents. Players #5 and #4 step in front of their rebound opponents and screen them away from the basket. Player #2 completes the rebounding triangle by moving in front of the basket. Player #3 moves in front of the shooter and screens him away from the basket. Player #1 is our exiting guard for the fast break.

Diagram 5-31 shows our alignment when we are shooting a free throw.

In Diagram 5-31 player #1 places himself two strides behind the first defensive rebounder. If the inside defensive rebounder screens #5 from the basket, #1 can cut freely to the basket for a rebound attempt.

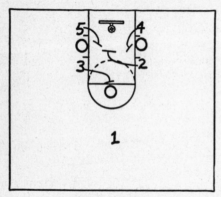

Diagram 5-30

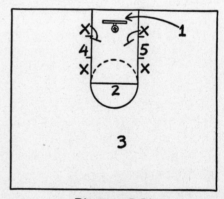

Diagram 5-31

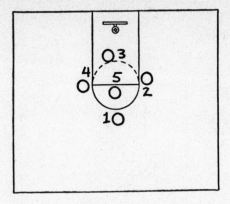

Diagram 5-32

Diagram 5-32 shows our basic alignment for jump ball situations.

We have evenly rotated our defenders around the center circle. Our players line up next to an opponent of similar height, speed, and quickness. If the jumpers are evenly matched, this is the alignment we use. Each of our players is alternately positioned between an opponent.

Diagram 5-33 shows our alignment if the opponent's jumper has a decided advantage.

All our defenders are placed in strong defensive positions that should eliminate all chances for the opponents to fast break and gain an easy basket. If we know the general direction in which the opponent's jumper usually tips or are able to pick up

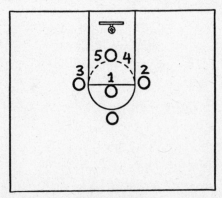

Diagram 5-33

their tipping plays, we would then arrange our players to attempt a steal of the ball on the tipoff.

Diagram 5-34 shows an adjustment from the strong defensive position for the reverse tip.

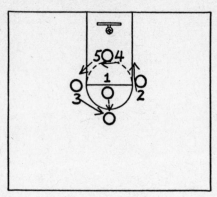

Diagram 5-34

STOPPING THE FAST BREAK

The fast break offense is extremely difficult to counter, but there are some techniques that can help disrupt the tempo of the fast break. Our first action is to concentrate on the rebounding area. The more second and third shots that our own offensive rebounders can garner, the harder it will be for the defense to quickly generate the fast break. We try to apply a great deal of pressure on the offensive board. This forces the defense to be more concerned with gaining control and/or possession of the ball.

In order to control the opponent's fast break, we must rely heavily on our scouting report. Here are some questions concerning the fast break that we need answered when analyzing the opponent's fast break:

1. Do the rebounders throw the exit pass to the man or an area?
2. Do the rebounders always throw the exit pass using the same technique repeatedly?
3. Should we fight the exit pass with one or two men?
4. Is it possible for our guards to intercept the exit pass?

5. What is their fast-break pattern?

6. Do they have a selected middle man to handle the ball on the fast break?

7. Do they ever fly a man deep and go for the long pass?

8. Can we draw the charging foul?

9. Do they fast break after a made basket or free throw? If so, what is the pattern?

10. Can we force the fast break to the side of the court?

After reading the scouting report and analyzing the answers to the preceding questions, we determine the way in which we'll defend against the fast break. We are flexible in our approach to defensing the break. As the questions indicate, our strategy will be reviewed and revised, depending on the opponent's ability level.

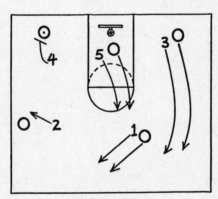

Diagram 5-35

Diagram 5-35 shows our defense of the controlled, traditional-type fast break. Player #4 moves in to fight the exit pass with his hands. This movement alone will help slow the break. If the defender can instinctively make the switch from offensive rebounder to defending the exit pass, our goal of disrupting the tempo of the fast break will be successful. Unfortunately, many teams let the opponents throw an uncontested exit pass. The defensive guards, #2 and #1, move to the exit lanes, positioning themselves for the interception or charge. If they can't make the interception, they should position themselves to defend the dribbler. Players #5 and #3 are hustling downcourt ahead of their men. They never jog down the floor beside their men; a smart offensive player will accelerate in the open court and get that all-important, one-step lead to the basket that will result in a score.

From our basic defense of the fast break that is shown in Diagram 5-25, we will make various coverage changes with our personnel as needed. We may have to send one guard deep and jam the middle with our weakside forward or center. We will do whatever works the best. The scouting report plays the vital role in how we will defense the fast break.

6

Special
Overplay-Pressure
Defense

PURPOSE OF IMPLEMENTATION

There are times when a zone defense completely destroys an opponent. The type of zone defense that we favor is a trapping one. This is a 1-3-1 pressuring defense played with several variations. This pressuring, trapping defense fits in well with our overall defensive philosophy of constant harassment. The offense will be forced to pass the basketball out of several double-team situations. The dribble will be totally taken away from the offensive team.

The double teams or traps will only be successful if the defenders can assume a right-angle position with their bodies in relation to the ball handler. The ball handler must never be allowed to dribble between these double-teaming defenders. Another key element in the success of a good double team is that the defenders shadow the ball with their hands in order to force a poor pass from the trap. This will greatly increase the opportunity for an interception. The longer a pass hangs, the greater the chance of an interception.

Some teams simply cannot handle those defenses that create double-team situations. Because of poor passing skills and the inability to cut to open areas, the 1-3-1 pressuring defense can be an extremely difficult problem for the offense to conquer. Any offense that lacks the proper ball-handling skills will find it very difficult to move the basketball in an effective manner. The defense will be able to force the offense into constant positions of disadvantage. Any successful defense must be able to control what the offense does with the basketball.

BASIC SET

Diagram 6-1 shows the basic set for the Overplay-Pressure 13 Defense at the three-quarter court area.

G_1 aligns himself between the offensive guards. G_2 positions for an eventual trap with G_1. F_3 is positioning himself to help discourage the pass to the middle man, #5. F_4 is playing the pass to the strongside forward, #3. C_5 is defending the basket against a lay-up and looking to intercept the pass to the weakside forward, #4.

OVERPLAY-PRESSURE 13 ASSIGNMENTS

Diagram 6-2 shows the dribbler being forced into a double-team situation.

The ball handler is forced up the side into a double team with G_1 and G_2. The man responsible for developing this double-team situation is G_1, the point man on the Overplay-Pressure 13 Defense. Let's analyze the responsibilities of G_2 and his teammates.

Responsibilities of the Point Defender, G_1

As shown in Diagram 6-2, G_1 aligns himself between the offensive guards. This is his first and most important positioning maneuver. He must prevent a quick, sharp pass from one guard to the other offensive guard. He is attempting to slow this pass and thus allow the defense to keep pace with the basketball. Every pass must be made over the head of the point defender which will help increase the hang time. If G_1 positions himself properly, the offensive guards, #1 and #2, will be forced to throw semi-lobs or get the pass deflected by G_1. Deflected and lobbed passes allow the defense to

a. shift before the pass is completed; therefore, no defensive weaknesses will be exposed, or,

b. intercept the lob or recover the deflected pass.

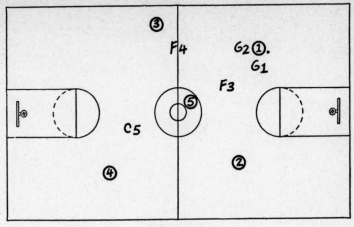

Diagram 6-1

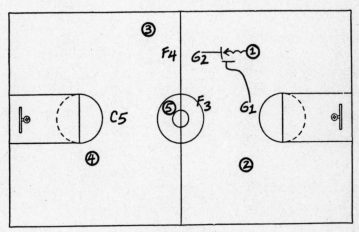

Diagram 6-2

If the point guard, G_1, allows the offensive guards to pass the basketball quickly to each other, they will have no problem in advancing the ball towards their basket. G_1 must be intelligent and hard working. He sets the tone for the entire defense.

G_1's next assignment is to force the ball handler up the side of the court and into the double team with the wing defender. In Diagram 6-2 the double team occurs in unison with G_2. If the passing situation from #1 to #2 is made difficult by G_1, a trap will often be forced on the dribbling #1.

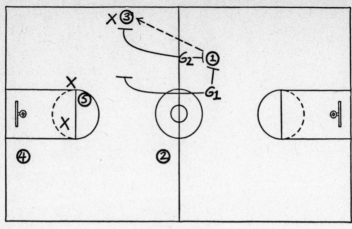

Diagram 6-3

Diagram 6-3 shows the pass from #1 to #3 and the shift of our point defender, G_1.

As demonstrated, player #1 is able to complete the pass to the strongside forward, #3. G_1 must quickly recover to the high-post area. His primary job is to prevent the pass to the high-post man. If this pass is prevented, the offensive team will not be able to attack to the weak side for an easy shot.

Diagram 6-4 shows the passing play G_1 is preventing by defending the high post.

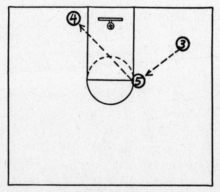

Diagram 6-4

As G_1 develops a feel for defending the high-post position, he may be able to intercept the return pass from #3 to #1. If there is no offensive center at the high post, he may begin to edge toward the strongside passing lane as shown in Diagram 6-5.

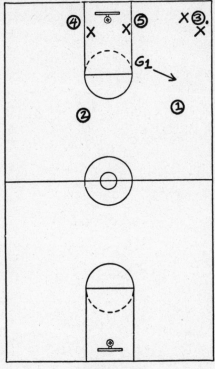

Diagram 6-5

Another opportunity may develop for the interception of the return pass, when the strongside forward, #3, quits trying to pass the basketball to the high post. Because of the fine coverage G_1 is giving this area, #3 simply begins returning the pass to #1 without thinking. G_1 should sense this situation developing and go for the interception.

Responsibilities of the Baseline Defender, F_4

Diagram 6-2 shows the baseline defender, F_4, defending at the three-quarter court area against #1, the offensive guard. He is playing for the interception of the pass from #1 to #3. He positions halfway between the side of the lane and the strongside forward. He is also higher towards the ball than #3, which gives the defender a better angle to the passing lane. F_4's job is to prevent the pass from #1 to #3 as often as possible. If he realizes that this pass cannot be intercepted, his next move is to prevent #3, the strongside offensive forward, from driving the baseline as shown in Diagram 6-6.

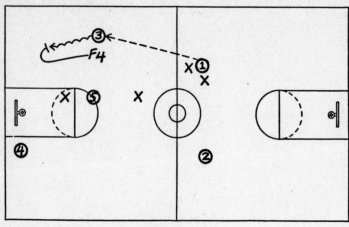

Diagram 6-6

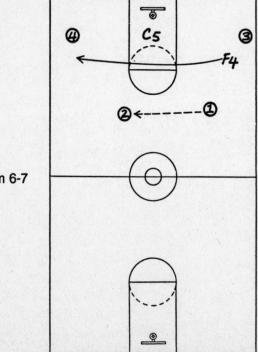

Diagram 6-7

Cutting off the baseline move of the strongside forward is mandatory. He cannot be allowed this penetration. A drive along the baseline would create a disadvantage for the inner defense. F_4 is to keep constant pressure on #3, halt his baseline penetration, and double-team player #3 with the wing man, G_2.

Diagram 6-7 shows the movement of the baseline defender, F_4, when the basketball is passed from #1 to #2.

F_4 crosses the court in front of C_5, not behind, and goes to the opposite side of the court. It is important that F_4 cuts in front of C_5 because it allows him to maintain good floor position on the new passing lane from #2 to #4. This will enable him to successfully deflect or intercept several attempted passes from #2 to #4.

Another responsibility for F_4 is to defend the baseline jump shot. He must be a real hustler and force the offensive forward to hurry his shot by rushing at him from his defensive position.

Responsibilities of the Wing Defender, G_2

The responsibilities for both wing defenders are the same. We shall concentrate on G_2. Diagram 6-2 shows G_2 setting himself for the trap on #1 with G_1, the point defender.

Diagram 6-8 shows that G_2 is positioned in the passing lane between #1 and #3. This is to force a lob pass over his head and hands. The chances of F_4 making an interception greatly increase when this type of pass is thrown.

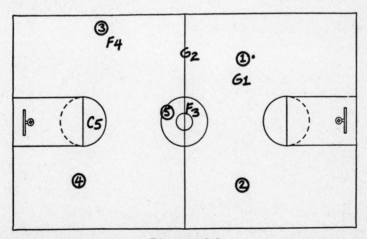

Diagram 6-8

G_2 is waiting just across the midcourt line for G_1 to force the dribbler to him. Once the dribbler comes within four feet of either side of the midcourt line, G_2 traps with G_1 as shown in Diagram 6-9.

In Diagram 6-10, #1 withstands the trap and passes to #3. G_2 turns and follows this pass and double-teams #3 with F_4, the baseline defender. Both defenders contest any attempted pass by #3 from the double team.

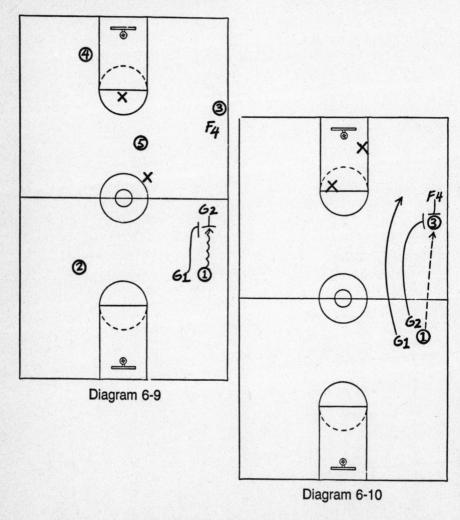

Diagram 6-9

Diagram 6-10

Diagram 6-11 shows the ball being passed from #1 to #2. G_2's immediate reaction to the weakside guard receiving the pass is to defend the high post or middle area. A successful pass from the guard, #2, to the center, #5, may result in an easy lay-up for #3 as shown in Diagram 6-12.

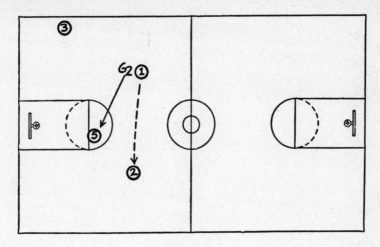

Diagram 6-11

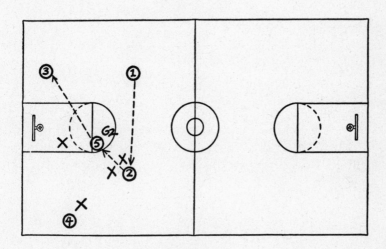

Diagram 6-12

Diagram 6-13 shows #2 continuing to move the basketball around the perimeter to #4 in the corner.

Once the ball has reached #4 in the far corner G_2 becomes the rebounder on the weak side. His only responsibility is to keep #3 from getting the easy weakside offensive rebound. This is vital.

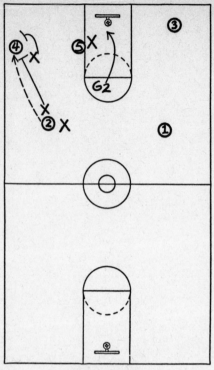

Diagram 6-13

Responsibilities of the Pivot Defender, C_5

The pivot defender, C_5, has the basic responsibility for defending the basket against lay-ups and short jump shots. When either offensive guard, #1 or #2, has the basketball, C_5 is

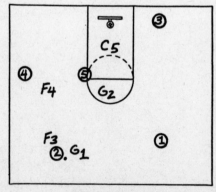

Diagram 6-14

responsible for discouraging the high-post jump shot. Diagram 6-14 shows this situation.

When the guard, #2, passes to the strongside forward, #4, the pivot defender, C_5, moves to the strongside low post to defend the basket. Diagram 6-15 shows this situation.

C_5 may play behind the offensive strongside low-post player, or he may play in front of him depending on the match-ups. If there is no offensive player at the strongside low post, C_5 may move into the mid-post area to help defend the high post as shown in Diagram 6-16.

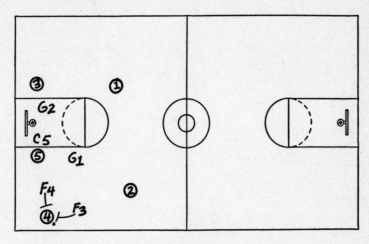

Diagram 6-15

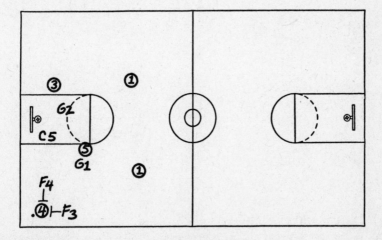

Diagram 6-16

VARIOUS SHIFTING PATTERNS

The Overload Shift

Diagram 6-17 shows the basic shift made when the opponents move the basketball to the forward position. Diagram 6-18 shows the defensive shift being altered into an overload. In this shift the weakside wing is responsible for defending the strongside low post. The pivot defender, C_5, now is responsible for defending the high post. This allows G_1 to float outside and seek a possible interception of a pass thrown from #2 to #1 or from #3 to #2. This is a very effective shift when the opponents attempt to flood the high- and low-post areas.

When the ball is passed from the guard position to the high post, our defenders simply drop to the basket. C_5 takes the high-post offensive player. The wings drop to the basket with F_4. The point defender, G_1, double-teams the post man with C_5. We try to force the basketball back to the outside.

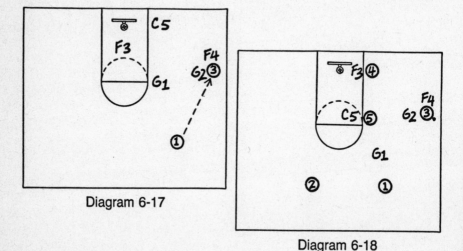

Diagram 6-17

Diagram 6-18

The Denial Shift

Diagram 6-19 depicts #1 being trapped.

Diagram 6-20 shows the pass from #1 to #3. The only change made here is that C_5 will continue to front the offensive center. F_3 has weakside rebounding responsibility unless #4, the weakside forward, moves to the strongside low post. F_3 would then defend this area. G_1 still has high-post responsibility if C_5 vacates the area with the offensive center.

The Denial Shift is very effective in stopping the offense from attacking our Overplay-Pressure 13 Defense at the center position. Many teams will attempt to get our defense shifting, then hit the high post who in turn feeds the ball to the low-post weak side for an easy shot. This will completely stop exploitation of the high-post play. The Denial Shift and Overload Shift are simple, yet effective, variations of a fine defense.

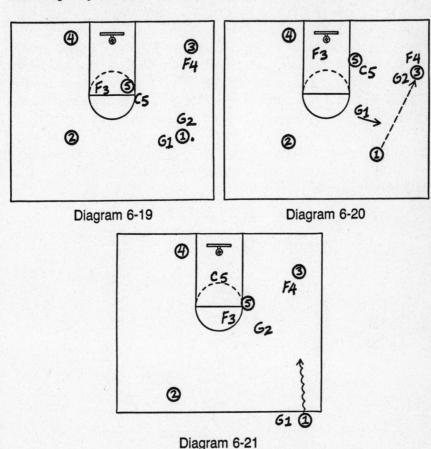

Diagram 6-19   Diagram 6-20

Diagram 6-21

HALF-COURT PRESSURE

Diagram 6-21 shows the Overplay-Pressure 13 Defense at the half-court level. The trap of #1 is delayed until he steps across the midcourt line. Sometimes we even wait until the dribbler has

advanced two or three full strides past the midcourt before we
attack with the trap or double team.

The advantage of holding the double team to the half-court
level is that the defense has much less area to cover than in the
full-court press. The players can cover their areas quicker, and
this is an important key to the success of any trapping defense.
The quicker the players can shift and anticipate, the better the
defense.

THREE-QUARTER COURT PRESSURE

Diagram 6-22 shows the Overplay-Pressure 13 Defense at the
three-quarter court mark. The offense allows the inbounds pass.
Pressure is first applied by G_1, the point defender, at the top of
the key. He slides in between the offensive guards and attempts
to force the ball handler up the side of the floor. The wings do not
apply the trap until the ball handler advances to the hash mark.
Again, delaying the trap helps to keep the defense from spread-
ing too thin. Everyone's assignments remain the same as in the
basic Overplay-Pressure 13 Defense.

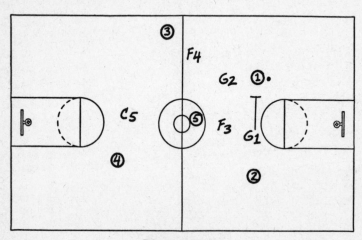

Diagram 6-22

QUARTER-COURT PRESSURE

The Overplay-Pressure 13 Defense played at the quarter
court is effective. This creates some unusual problems for the

opposition. It breeds indecision among the offensive players; they become unsure of when to pass and when to shoot. The traps of this fine defense vary depending on each situation.

We have named this phase of our Overplay-Pressure 13 Defense the "Quick Trap."

Diagram 6-23 shows the initial set position of our quick-trap defense. The dotted lines represent the shooting range of the opponents. We do not trap the opponents beyond their shooting range. Outside of this area, we play the defense as a regular 1-3-1 zone.

When #1 advances into the shooting area, as shown in Diagram 6-24, the defense then traps the basketball with G_1 and G_2. Until the point of the defensive attack, #1 has been the responsibility of G_1.

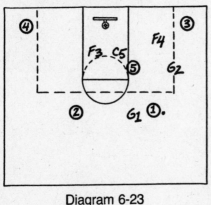

Diagram 6-23

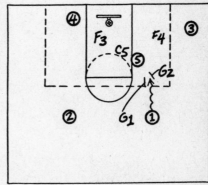

Diagram 6-24

Diagram 6-25 shows #3 with the basketball in the shooting area. The defensive assignments are the same as in our basic Overplay-Pressure 13 Defense.

Diagram 6-26 shows #3 with the basketball outside the shooting area. In this situation F_4 takes #3 one-on-one, and G_2 drops to help defend the mid- and high-post areas.

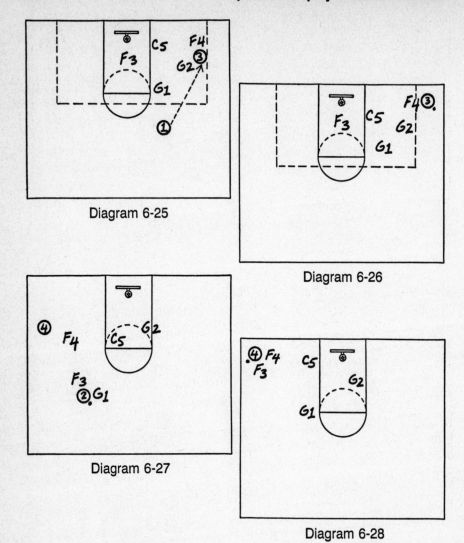

Diagram 6-25

Diagram 6-26

Diagram 6-27

Diagram 6-28

The Quick Trap can also be adjusted to double-team one or two shooters.

Diagrams 6-27 and 6-28 show the defense trapping #2 and #4 only. The remainder of the offensive players are met with a standard 1-3-1 zone as shown in Diagram 6-29 and 6-30.

When practicing the Quick Trap, we usually chalk the trap areas on the floor. Our players then know exactly in what areas the trapping will occur. If we are trapping selected players who key the scoring, we simulate the trapping situations that will be faced in the actual game.

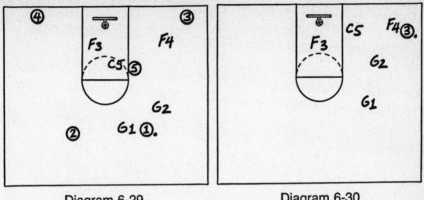

Diagram 6-29   Diagram 6-30

This is an outstanding defense, and we would recommend the quarter-court phase of the Overplay-Pressure 13 Defense. Even a team lacking defensive quickness is capable of playing this type of defense because of the limited defensive territory defended.

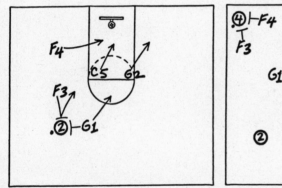

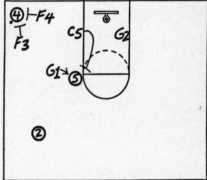

Diagram 6-31   Diagram 6-32

REBOUNDING PLANS

Diagram 6-31 shows the rebounding assignments when the opposition takes a shot from the guard position #2.

C_5 will rebound the middle. F_4 and G_2 have responsibility on their respective sides, and the rebounding triangle is formed.

Diagram 6-32 shows the shot being taken from the corner.

C_5 will move to the middle of the lane when the shot is taken. G_2 rebounds the weak side. F_4 and F_3 rebound on the strong side. Again, the rebounding triangle is formed.

7

Full-Court
Overplay-Pressure
Man-Man Defense

OVERVIEW OF THE COMPLETE FULL-COURT
SYSTEM

The players call our full-court overplay-pressure defensive system the Confusion Defense. This phase of our defense has been very effective in giving the offensive team several problems to solve. Even though they may have decided what defensive switches we make, the real problem is for their players to make the correct decisions under pressure to counter our defensive adjustments.

Simply stated, our Confusion Defense utilizes the man-to-man, 2-2-1, and 1-2-2 full-court presses. When the opponents have the basketball out-of-bounds, our defense is set in a full-court man-to-man press, attempting to intercept the inbounds pass. When the offense completes the inbounds pass, our defense may react any one of the three following ways:

1. Change to a 2-2-1 full-court zone press.
2. Change to a 1-2-2 full-court zone press.
3. Remain in the man-to-man full-court press.

As the basketball is advanced across the midcourt line and beyond the hash mark, our defense undergoes a third change of character. We switch into our half-court man-to-man overplay.

We are attempting to force each offensive player to hurry, both physically and mentally. We pressure the inbounds pass, attempting to force a five-second count. Once the basketball is on the court, our concept of changing defenses causes the opponents to dribble against the zone presses and pass against the man-to-man press. By keeping pressure on the opponents the instant they take the ball out-of-bounds, the less chance there will be for allowing the offensive players to understand the defense. Played with intensity, this defense can be devastating.

BASELINE-TO-BASELINE DEFENSE

The first phase of our presses is the full-court man-to-man. This press is the backbone of the Confusion Defensive System. The Confusion System will fail if a poor man-man defense is played at both the full- and half-court levels. The drills that we discussed in earlier chapters must be executed perfectly during the actual game for the Confusion Defense to function successfully.

We begin teaching the man-to-man press as a total defense from the time the opponents take the basketball out-of-bounds until they shoot. It is an extension of our half-court man-to-man. We like to think that our half-court defense with one or two men sagging on the weak side and the Ball Red are simply half-court man-to-man presses. Thus, it is not too difficult to move our half-court defense to the full-court level.

Side Push Set

Diagram 7-1 shows the set for our full-court man-to-man press. Each defensive player is attempting to deny his man the basketball. G_1 is guarding the passer tightly. He attempts to deflect the inbounds pass or force a lob pass to be thrown, increasing the chance for an interception.

G_2 is playing in a Side Push Set position. He is in an overplay position on the offensive man's outside hip, forcing him to the weak side of the court. This creates a longer inbounds pass and increases the chance for an interception by G_2. Diagram 7-2 shows G_2's foot positioning.

Diagram 7-2 indicates G_2 has taken the weak side of the court away from the receiver. Once the receiver begins his cut away to the strong side, it becomes a foot race to catch the pass. G_2 has increased his chance for an interception because he knows the basic direction of the receiver's cut.

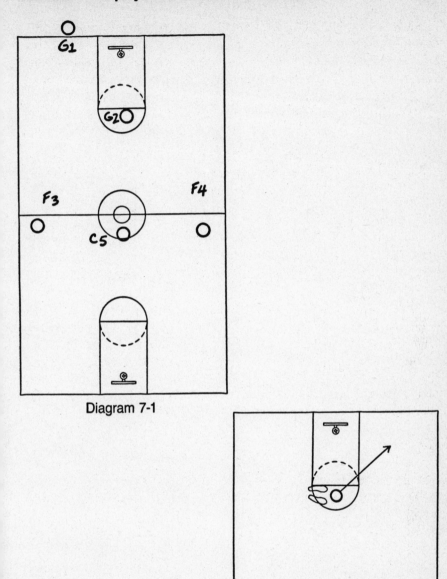

Diagram 7-1

Diagram 7-2

F_3, F_4, and C_5 assume their normal overplay position, adjusting their distance to the man guarded depending on where the basketball is. Each player must always see his man and the basketball simultaneously. They must work for the interception, deflection, or five-second count on the inbounds passing situation.

Once the ball is inbounded, the man guarding the dribbler makes him change directions with his dribble as he advances up the court. If the ball handler picks up the dribble, we immediately go into our Ball Red Defense.

We never allow a defender to trot downcourt if his man has gotten around him. He always runs to the level of the basketball or below and regains his man or helps defend the basket.

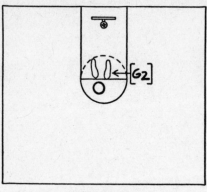

Diagram 7-3

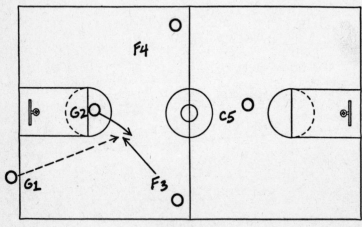

Diagram 7-4

Front-Up Set

Diagram 7-3 shows the alignment in a Front-Up Set. The only change is that G₂ is now fronting the inbounds receiver. He denies any cut toward the basketball, forcing the receiver to break downcourt to free himself for the inbounds pass. F_3, F_4, and C_5 should be extra alert and be ready to help defend this inbounds situation. Diagram 7-4 shows the development of this play.

Floater-Safe Set

After practicing the first two sets, our players learn how difficult it is to defend the long backdoor passes. They begin to understand what the terms "hustle" and "recovery" mean. Once they have learned the positioning in the first two sets, we organize our full-court man-to-man press the way it will best complement the zone presses in the Confusion System. Our players, especially the guard, G_2, defending the inbounds receiver, must have a good feel for the two sets. Diagram 7-5 shows the alignment.

G_1 has been moved to a floater position. C_5 goes deep to defend the basket. G_2 may align in a Side Push Set. F_3 and F_4 remain in their overplay positions.

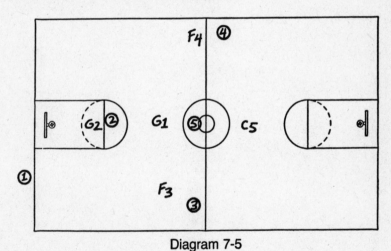

Diagram 7-5

VARYING DEFENSIVE ASSIGNMENTS

The defensive assignments for our man-to-man press depend on each player's ability to think quickly as an individual and as a team. The defense must work intensely, displaying the highest degree of teamwork.

The individual responsibilities pertinent to the man-to-man press with the floater are as follows:

1. G_1 plays the floater position at the top of the key. He is responsible for helping G_2 with the backdoor lob that is thrown into his area. As shown in Diagram 7-6, G_1 also has responsibility to prevent #5, the offensive center, from receiving a direct pass from out-of-bounds in the middle of the court. Additionally, he attempts to keep #5 from cutting below the foul line, as shown in Diagram 7-7. Depending on the ability of the opponents to get

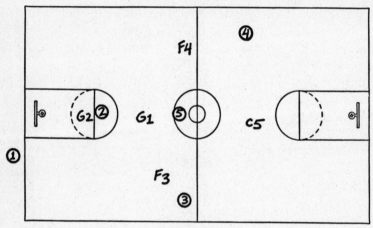

Diagram 7-6

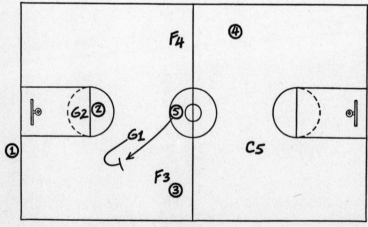

Diagram 7-7

through our combination presses, G_1 sometimes will deny #5 the ball all the way to the baseline. At other times he will contain #5 until he moves to within 12 feet of the baseline.

Once the basketball is in play, G_1 drops back to the top of the key and picks up the out-of-bounds guard, #1, one-on-one as shown in Diagram 7-8. By returning quickly to the middle of the half court, G_1 helps prevent exploitation of this area.

2. G_2 may use either the side push or the front push. G_2 usually starts playing #2 on the side and then mixes in the front push. His job is to prevent #2 from receiving the

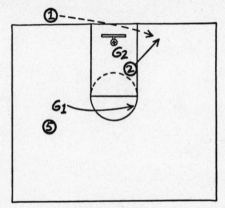

Diagram 7-8

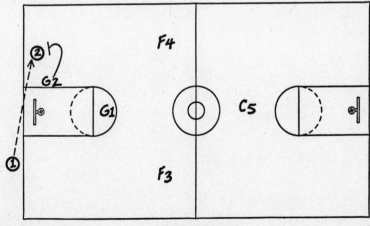

Diagram 7-9

inbounds pass. Once #2 does receive the inbounds pass, G_2 must quickly regain his defensive position ahead of #2 and then attempt to turn the dribbler. This action is drawn in Diagram 7-9.

3. The defensive assignments of F_3 and F_4 are identical. F_3 assumes an overplay position to the inside of the court, favoring the basketball. F_4, who is positioned on the weak side, favors the middle of the court, and the basketball a little more than does F_3. Diagram 7-10 shows this alignment.

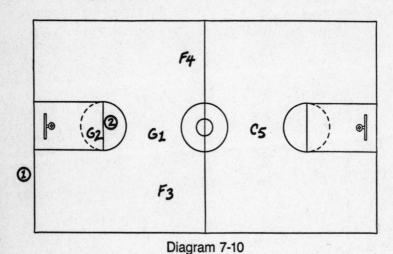

Diagram 7-10

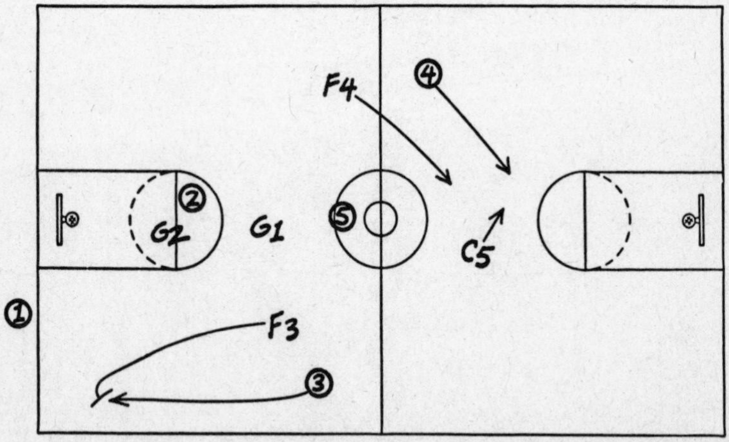

Diagram 7-11

F_2 and F_4 are to deny their men the basketball all the way to the baseline. They will also defend the backdoor pass from out-of-bounds as their men break towards the opponent's basket. They defend the backdoor until they reach the opponent's offensive hash mark. At that time, they release their men to C_5 for defense of the long pass. Both these situations are shown in Diagram 7-11 with F_3 defending the baseline and F_4 defending deep with C_5.

4. C_5 has major responsibility for defending the long pass downcourt and preventing the easy lay-up shot by the offense. C_5 will follow his man to the midcourt line while helping defend the inbounds pass from #1. Once C_5's man advances across the midcourt line and towards the out-of-

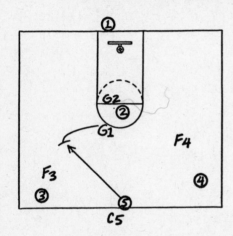

Diagram 7-12

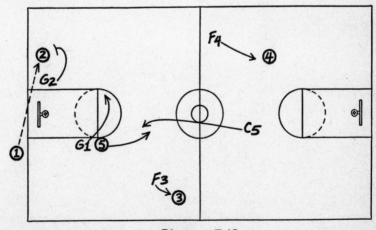

Diagram 7-13

bounds passer, G_1 assumes responsibility for preventing the pass from going to this player. Once the inbounds pass has been completed, C_5 moves up court to pick up #5 man-to-man. Diagrams 7-12 and 7-13 show these situations.

5. Once the basketball is inbounded, all defenders assume responsibility for their men.

DOUBLE-UP SITUATIONS

In Diagram 7-14, #2 has caught the inbounds pass and is beating G_2 down the sideline. G_1, who is positioned in the middle, moves over to double-team #2 and stop his penetration. F_3 moves to the middle of the court to look for the interception of a pass to #5 or #1. If and when #2 completes a pass out of the double team, our defenders get downcourt and pick up their assigned players as quickly as possible. Of course, the ball handler is covered immediately.

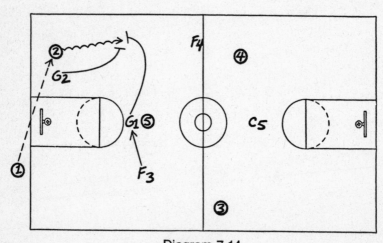

Diagram 7-14

Diagram 7-15 shows another possible double-team situation. Player #3 has accepted a pass with his back turned to the defense. F_3 and G_1 double-team, while G_2 plays the potential pass to #1 or #2. F_4 moves in to the middle and plays the possibility of a pass to #5 or #2. C_5 defends the pass downcourt to the basket. We are playing to intercept the pass thrown by #3. If we don't intercept, our defenders hustle downcourt and get into their man-to-man half-court defense.

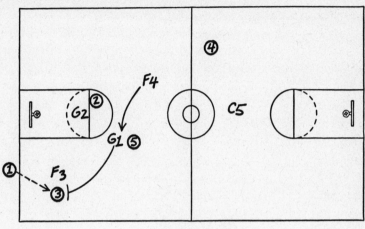

Diagram 7-15

DRILLS

3-2 Full-Court Drill

Diagram 7-16 shows G_2 fronting #2, forcing him towards the ten-second line. F_3 is defending the strongside forward, denying him the crosscourt cut and forcing him against the sideline. G_1 is

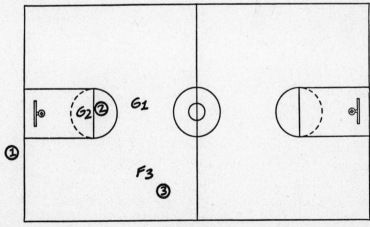

Diagram 7-16

in the floater position, helping G_2 with the backdoor lob pass. He may also help F_3 with this same pass. G_1 plays for the interception of the inbounds pass as well as setting up for the charging foul from #2 or #3 as they cut downcourt looking for the backdoor lob pass. A rule that is followed in this drill is that the inbounds pass may not be thrown across the ten-second line.

When the pass is inbounded, G_1 picks up #1 man-to-man as he approaches the foul line. G_1 must first know that G_2 has regained a fundamental guarding position on #2 before he leaves the middle. If #2 has the basketball and G_2 is out of position, allowing the downcourt penetration, G_1 would move to cover #2, and G_2 would switch to #1. Diagrams 7-17 and 7-18 show these situations.

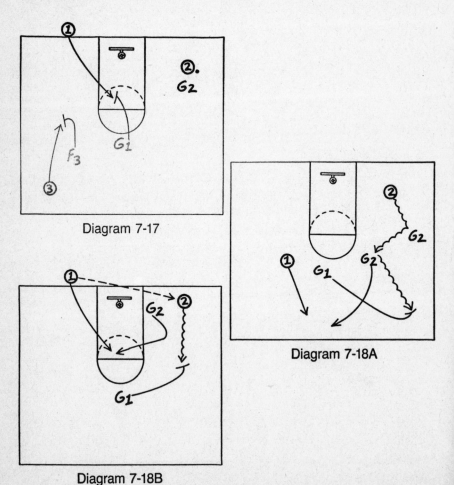

Diagram 7-17

Diagram 7-18A

Diagram 7-18B

4-4 Full-Court Drill

Diagram 7-19 shows our defense in a man-to-man press situation with all the defenders using the overplay defensive technique. G_2 is on the side of #2, forcing him to the weakside corner. F_3 and F_4 are denying their men the crosscourt cut and forcing them to the sideline. G_1 has moved to the out-of-bounds passer, fighting the attempted pass with his hands. G_1 may, instead, place himself in the floater position also. When G_1 is in the floater position, the overplay positions of G_2, F_3, and F_4 do not change. We prefer the overplay side push position for G_2 because he will rarely get beaten by the dribble once his man accepts the inbounds pass. There will be fewer situations when G_1 and G_2 must switch offensive men. Again, the inbounds pass must not be thrown across the ten-second line.

When the first pass is completed, a game of 4-4 ensues. The defenders use their fundamentals in guarding the ball handler and the other men without the ball. It is imperative that the dribbler never gets around his defensive guard on the man-to-man press. The defender must turn the dribbler repeatedly without allowing the penetration.

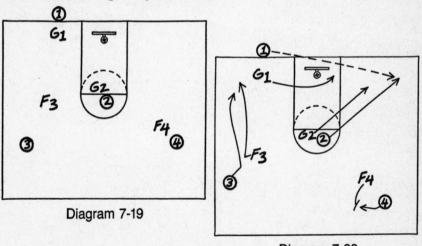

Diagram 7-19

Diagram 7-20

Diagram 7-20 shows #2 breaking to the weakside corner and G_2 working to maintain his overplay position. G_1 is fighting the inbounds pass with his hands. F_3 and F_4 are seen denying the crosscourt cut, forcing their men down the sideline.

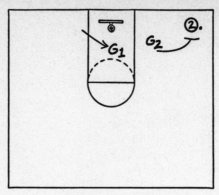

Diagram 7-21

In Diagram 7-21, G_2 quickly moves to his turn-the-dribbler position when #2 accepts the inbounds pass.

5-4 Full-Court Drill

Diagram 7-22 shows the alignment for our 5-4 Full-Court Drill. The difference between this drill and the 4-4 Full-Court Drill is that an offensive center (#5) is added. He remains in the game until the inbounds pass is completed. Once the ball is inbounded, #5 leaves the court and a full-court man-to-man press game takes place.

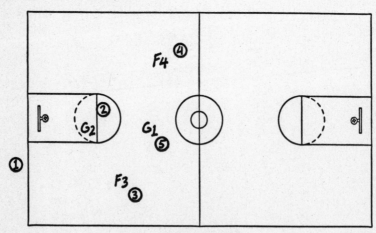

Diagram 7-22

3-3 Denial Full-Court Overplay Drill

Diagram 7-23 shows the 3-3 drill alignment. During the season we will encounter some teams that will align two men on the foul line and then screen for each other in order to complete the inbounds pass. Our defenders, G_2 and G_3 assume overplay positions on #2 and #3. This alignment is shown in Diagram 7-23.

If the offensive players use the screen-and-roll play as they so often do, we move G_2 and G_3 to the inside of the offensive players, forcing them to the sideline. Diagram 7-24 shows the new defensive alignment of G_2 and G_3.

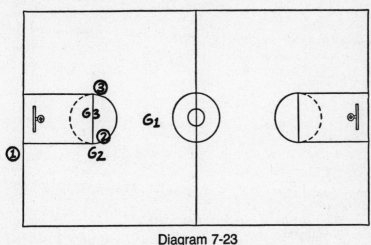

Diagram 7-23

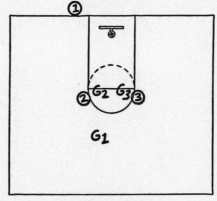

Diagram 7-24

G₁ in these diagrams has assumed the floater position. When G₁ is in the floater position, G₂ and G₃ may use a third defensive alignment versus #2 and #3. They may front both offensive players, forcing them away from the basketball. G₁ then plays for the backdoor lob downcourt. Diagram 7-25 shows this alignment.

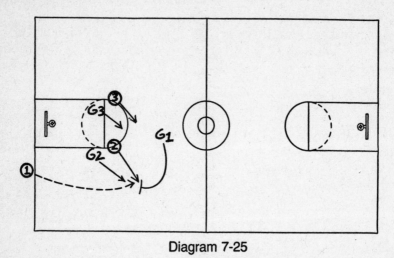

Diagram 7-25

3-3 Center Jump Drill

Diagram 7-26 shows the initial formation for our 3-3 Center Jump Drill. The coach tosses up the basketball and a three-on-

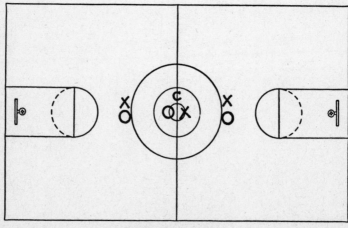

Diagram 7-26

three, full-court, man-to-man game takes place. Both teams play a man-to-man press. The first team to score three baskets wins. All the defensive fundamentals are applied in this quick, intense hustling drill. This is an outstanding drill to improve physical conditioning and to teach defensive recovery. It also enhances each player's ability to get up and down the floor quickly. If a defensive player is beaten in the open court, he learns the importance of hustling back to the basket as his teammates cover his defensive lapse.

2-2 Full-Court Overplay Drill

Diagram 7-27 shows the alignment for our 2-2 Full-Court Drill. The inbounds pass may not be thrown across the midcourt line. G_2 sets in the overplay position between his man and the basketball, forcing him to the weakside corner. G_1 is fighting the inbounds pass with his hand. Once the inbounds pass is thrown to an offensive man, a game of two-on-one takes place until a basket is scored by one of the teams.

1-1 Full-Court Overplay Drill

Diagram 7-28 shows our one-on-one drill. The offensive player begins by advancing the basketball from the baseline to the free throw line. Once he reaches the foul line, the defender may attack. A full-court game takes place until one basket is scored.

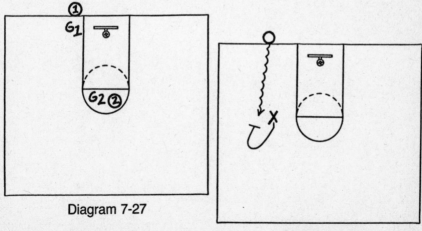

Diagram 7-27

Diagram 7-28

8

Overplay-Pressure Man-to-Man Full-Court Defense and the 2-2-1 Press

Chapter 7 discussed the Overplay-Pressure Man-Man Full-Court Press with the floater, G_1, and the goal tender, C_5, as shown in Diagram 8-1.

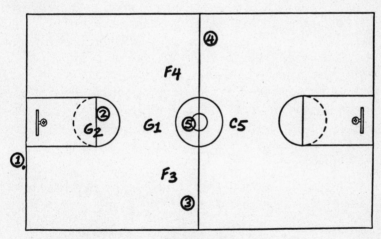

Diagram 8-1

In review, we set the man-to-man press until the inbounds pass is completed. Then our defense must decide whether to stay with this particular type press or switch to some type of a zone press. The zone press that we can most easily switch to is the 2-2-1. This press complements the man-to-man press quite well.

Once the offense becomes accustomed to dribbling downcourt, we will switch into the 2-2-1 zone press. Once the inbounds pass is completed, we would switch from the man-to-man to the 2-2-1 zone press and force the dribbler up the sideline toward the ten-second line. We then look for the trap at the intersection of the ten-second line and the sideline. The dribbler is often very startled to find himself in a trapping situation.

SIGNAL SYSTEM OF CALLING DEFENSE

Hand Signals

When we began combining the man-to-man and 2-2-1 presses, a system for switching the defense had to be worked out. We have used two signal systems for calling the defensive switches. The first is to let our floater call the defensive switches by using body signals. As soon as we score, our defenders look to the floater for the type of defenses we will play. If the floater has both hands below his waist, we will remain in the man-to-man press all the way downcourt. If the floater has both hands over his head, we begin with our man-to-man press and then switch to a 2-2-1 zone press after the inbounds pass has been completed. We will use the 2-2-1 zone press until the ball is advanced about six feet past the midcourt line. At this point we switch to our half-court overplay man-to-man defense.

We choose the floater to call the defensive switches because of his centrally located position on the press. All the defenders can quickly see him as they move to their defensive positions.

Number Signals

The other signal system that we use is the number system. The floater or the coach could call out the number of the proper defense.

MAN-TO-MAN ROTATION TO THE 2-2-1 PRESS

Guard Rotation

Diagram 8-2 shows the rotation from the man-to-man to the 2-2-1 press. Player #1 inbounds to #2. G_2 slides in front of #2 and plays him just like he would in the man-man press. We must keep the pressure on the ball handler and not allow him to start looking at the defense. We want him to continue to think that we are still in the man-man press. G_1 does his best to discourage the shallow pass to the middle, and yet fake man-man responsibility in regards to #1. This should help to confuse the ball handler, #2.

Forward Rotation

F_3 and F_4 are also working as a tandem. F_3 takes the middle when the pivot player is in the deep middle. G_1 has responsibility for the shallow middle. F_4 sets up at the midcourt line, cutting the passing lane to #4.

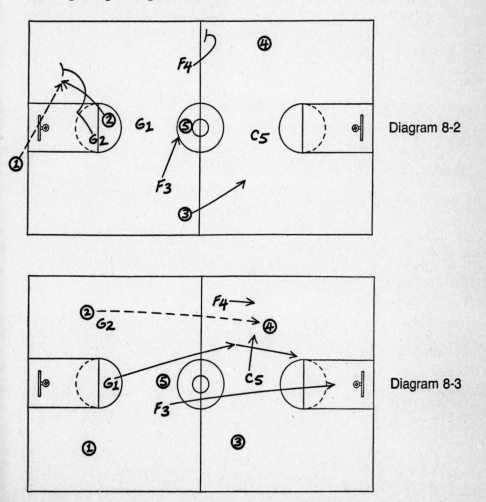

Diagram 8-2

Diagram 8-3

Center Rotation

C_5 has responsibility for the deep pass downcourt. He is looking for the crosscourt pass to #3 or the deep corner pass to #4 as shown in Diagram 8-3.

The Deep Corner Pass

Player #2 passes to #4 in the deep corner. F_4 has dropped one step below the midcourt line and forces the passer to lob the ball over his head. He does not allow a sharply thrown pass. By stepping below the midcourt line, F_4 forces #4 to go deeper downcourt. This increases the length of #2's pass and allows C_5 an excellent opportunity for the interception. F_3 must hustle to the basket and cover the potential pass from #4 to #3. G_1 hustles back to the basket, attempting to cover the potential pass from #4 to #5. F_4 and G_2 also hustle back downcourt.

Forward-Guard Trap

Diagram 8-4 shows the ball handler #2 advancing the basketball down the side rather than passing down the side to #4. F_4 waits until #2 nears the midcourt line and then moves up for the double team with G_2 in the coffin corner.

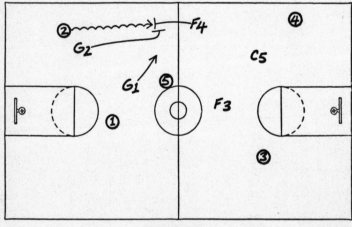

Diagram 8-4

G$_1$ moves to the level of the basketball, looking first for the pass to #5 in the middle and then the pass to #1. F$_3$ drops downcourt looking for the pass to #5 if he goes deep. F$_3$ is also ready to help C$_5$ with the deep corner pass to #4 or the crosscourt pass to #3. C$_5$ remains near the top of the key, attempting to read the pass from #2.

Stopping Up the Seam

If #2 gets ahead of his defender going down the sideline, he may hit #3 with a crosscourt pass. He will throw the pass before #4 can close in the double team. G$_2$ must stay ahead and not ride the dribbler's hip.(See Diagram 8-5.)

We instruct our guards not to intentionally force the dribbler down the sideline. The defender, G$_2$, should use the regular turn-the-dribbler technique. Because of the position of the weakside guard, the ball handler will eventually go to the sideline on his own.

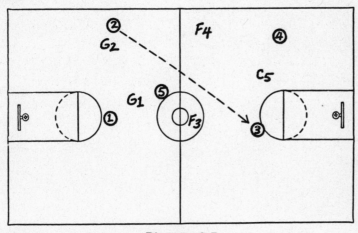

Diagram 8-5

Diagram 8-6 shows the defensive shifts when #2 passes to #1. G$_1$ will move out to the middle to play the ball handler one-on-one. G$_2$ quickly goes to the shallow middle to replace G$_1$. F$_3$ moves from the deep middle to the midcourt line. F$_4$ rushes into the deep middle replacing F$_3$. C$_5$ remains the safety or goaltender defending the basket. Diagram 8-7 shows the defensive arrangement when the shift has been completed.

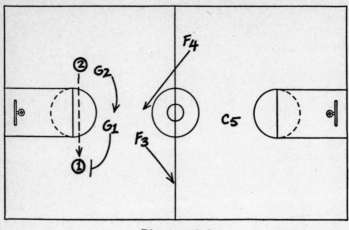

Diagram 8-6

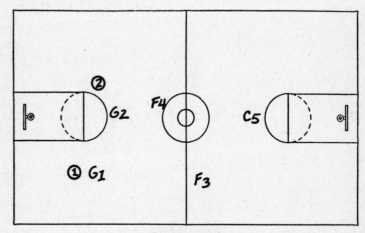

Diagram 8-7

Guard Dribbler Cross

If the ball handler does not realize that he is facing a 2-2-1 zone press, he may dribble diagonally across the floor. In Diagram 8-8, G_2 stays with his man as they move across the court. G_2 and G_1 have simply switched sides of the press. The offensive guards will continue to think that we are in a man-to-man press.

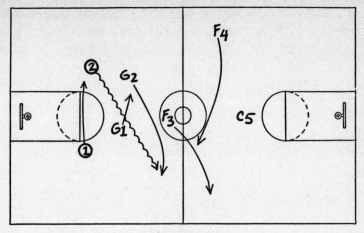

Diagram 8-8

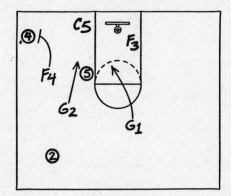

Diagram 8-9

2-2-1 PRESS TO THE HALF-COURT OVERPLAY-PRESSURE MAN-MAN DEFENSE

Diagram 8-9 shows #4 with the basketball after receiving the pass from #2. C_5 has started toward #4; he slows his advance until F_4 recovers to his man. G_2, G_1, and F_3 hustle back towards the lane to jam the basket and then they return to their assigned men in the man-man defense.

Initial Alignment

Because our initial alignment begins with the man-man full-court press, our players begin each series with their assigned man. Even though we may then switch into a 2-2-1 press when the basketball is inbounded, our defenders are always in the general area of their assigned men. This makes switching back to a half-court man-man defense from the full-court 2-2-1 zone press relatively simple.

C_5 plays a key role in helping us set up our man-man at half court. He must slow down the advance of the basketball, keeping the offense from penetrating to the basket. A shot blocker playing this position will be very effective in forcing the offense to hesitate.

Pressing After a Missed Shot

On occasion we will set up the 2-2-1 zone press after a missed shot. If a team appears to be weak against the zone press, we will press intensely at the three-quarter court after a missed shot. This often can be a devastating adjustment if the opponent has trouble getting organized during transition situations. Many teams simply jog downcourt after a missed shot, giving little thought to the total situation. The offensive players are usually only thinking about their half-court offense. They fail to remember that the game of basketball is played baseline to baseline at all times.

Diagram 8-10 shows the 2-2-1 zone press. G_1 covers the ball handler with a pressuring one-one defense. His assignment is to slow down the ball handler's advance, allowing his teammates to hustle back to their defensive positions. G_2 and F_4 must defend the middle quickly in order to stop penetration into the heart of the defense. C_5 must go all-out to get downcourt and defend the long pass and short jump shot. F_3 will cover the strong side. The secret is to get the defense arranged or in place as quickly as possible and disallow the ball handler's penetration of the zone. G_1, as shown in Diagram 8-10, must turn the dribbler and not allow him to operate without being pressured. If he can keep the ball handler laboring with the dribble, his defensive teammates will have time to set themselves.

At the half-court level, we return to our man-man defense. We follow the same procedure here as when switching from the zone press after a made basket.

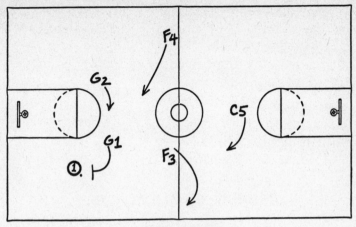

Diagram 8-10

Playing All Positions

The entire Confusion System is much more effective if all the defenders are capable of functioning at each position. We feel that the forwards should be able to fill the defensive guard positions, and the guards should be able to fill the forward slots when necessary. It is virtually impossible to maintain a textbook defensive set during all situations. The press becomes much more effective if all five players can interchange positions. This becomes extremely important in the three-quarter court 2-2-1 zone press when the players get caught out of position during a transition.

Forwards at Another Position

Having both forwards at the guard position changes the character of the entire press. Passes thrown by the offensive guards become more difficult to complete. Our bigger forwards, playing the front of the 2-2-1 zone press, cause problems for the offensive guards. Accustomed to playing against defenders their own size, the offensive guards must make several adjustments in their ball-handling and passing techniques. More lob passes will be thrown, which is to our defensive advantage.

By moving the quicker and more mobile guards to the forward spots, we also create another change in the press. More interceptions may occur because of the guard's speed in getting to the passing lanes.

Center and Guards at Another Position

A guard or forward may also have to play C_5's position in the 2-2-1 press at times. C_5, in turn, should be familiar with the duties at the guard or forward spots. He may be forced to fill either of them temporarily. Having five interchangeable defenders at our disposal is a positive factor.

PERSONNEL CHARACTERISTICS

Guards

Hustle and hard work are the two most important ingredients that the guards can possess. They must be able to keep constant pressure on their counterparts. Quickness of both hand and foot are very important qualities that should help them cover the necessary amount of ground. They must also understand how to anticipate the offensive man's next potential move. Guards in the range of 5'9" to 6'0" are ideal for these positions.

Forwards

The forwards should range in height from 6'0" to 6'4". They must possess quick feet. If they have the ability to anticipate in the open court, their effectiveness in double-teaming and intercepting passes would be greatly enhanced. These players should be naturally aggressive players.

Center

The center should be an outstanding jumper in the 6'4" or more range. He should be able to anticipate the pass and possess the ability to defend the basket against the drive or short jump shot. He must be able to intimidate the shooter near the basket. Being an aggressive, physical rebounder is another necessary ingredient to the effectiveness of the center.

INDIVIDUAL ASSIGNMENTS

Special Guard Assignments (G_2)

On the inbounds pass G_2 will be playing on the side of his man 80 to 90 percent of the time. This is a more fundamental position than fronting the inbounds offensive guard. G_2 only goes to the front push when we see that the momentum is swinging in our favor, and we try to move for some quick interceptions by increasing the pressure.

Diagram 8-11 shows the foot alignment of G_1 defending the inbounds offensive guard. G_2 attempts to encourage the offensive guard, #1, to make his cut to the sideline corner by positioning on the hip of #1. If G_2 does not take the strong side of the court away, #1 would then have a choice of cutting in any direction, and he becomes an open receiver quite easily. Therefore, G_2 forces his man to the weak side which increases the chance of an intercepted pass by the defense. G_2 is looking for the interception or deflection on all inbounds passes.

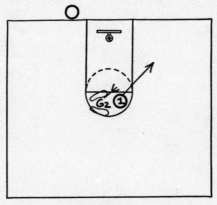

Diagram 8-11

When G_2 is practicing his denial of the inbounds pass, the coach makes G_2 repeat his denial positioning until he prevents the inbounds receiver from accepting the pass for a minimum of three seconds. We want all of our players going all-out to force the five-second violation on the inbounds pass. We can create a state of mental panic among the opponents by forcing the official's count to reach near five seconds on each out-of-bounds play. Eventually, the opposition will be more concerned with getting the basketball in play rather than analyzing our defense.

Diagram 8-12 shows the foot position of G_2 after the inbounds guard receives the pass. G_2 must decide whether to go for the interception or to establish position and allow the reception to be made. He cannot make unrealistic, unsound attempts to intercept every inbounds pass because this will result in his man receiving the ball and dribbling downcourt uncontested. Our defense will be extremely weak if G_2 cannot make intelligent decisions concerning attempted interceptions and body positioning after a reception.

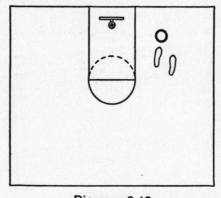

Diagram 8-12

Diagram 8-12 shows G_2 in ideal position to defense the ball handler. He has attained his guarding position on the opposite side from his original denial alignment. He has conceded the inbounds pass and must now pressure the ball handler quite intently to prevent him from recognizing the switch from the man-man to the 2-2-1 zone press.

G_2's job is the toughest of all the defenders' positions and possibly the most important. His behavior keys the tempo for the entire defense. He inspires his teammates with hard, aggressive play.

Guard Foot Positions (G_1 and G_2)

Diagram 8-13 shows the exact positioning of our defensive guard. G_2 has positioned the ball handler a half-body to his strong side. He does not encourage the dribbler up the side. He turns him as often as possible.

G_1, the weakside guard, does not use the open stance as is customary in the traditional zone press defense. He remains in the man-man overplay straddle stance, positioning himself halfway between the shallow post player and weakside offensive guard. We hope that the offensive guards will have more difficulty in recognizing the defense.

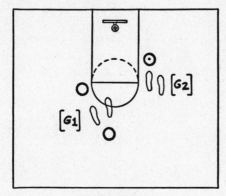

Diagram 8-13

Forward Foot Position

Diagram 8-14 shows the foot and body positioning of our strongside and weakside forwards. Both players are using the straddle stance. This action will help conceal our defense, giving it the appearance of our man-man press. This creates confusion for the opponents.

F_4 must force the strongside offensive forward downcourt. By using the straddle stance, he is able to check the offensive man's cut toward the basketball. He does not leave the straddle overplay positioning until he advances for the double team with G_2 at the coffin corner.

F_3 will continue to maneuver from the straddle overplay stance on the weak side. He has shifted to the deep middle to help cover the potential pass to the center of the court. From his straddle stance he is capable of moving quickly either forward or backward.

C_5 has positioned himself in a parallel stance. He is anticipating the long, downcourt pass to either offensive forward. He must not take any foolish chances at an interception. If he misses the interception, the forward will be able to drive to the basket for a high percentage shot. To intercept the long pass, C_5 must position himself high enough to maintain a good cutting angle to the passing lane of the intended receiver. C_5's floor positioning will depend on his quickness and reaction ability.

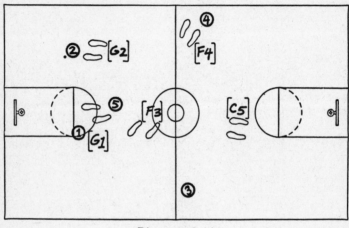

Diagram 8-14

Diagram 8-15 shows C_5's positioning on the side of the lane. He surmised that he had no chance for the interception, so he is now goal-tending or defending the basket and not committing himself to the outside of the court. He positions himself between the offensive players and the basket. He places the decision-making process on the offense. They must slow down and determine how to attack. C_5 wants to force a jump shot over his outstretched hand rather than allow a lay-up shot. He also wants to slow the offensive attack in hopes of allowing his defensive teammates ample time to help defend the basket.

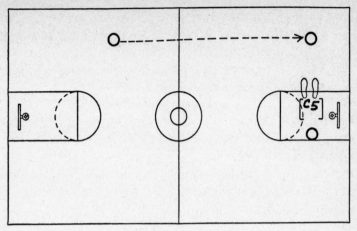

Diagram 8-15

Press Drill

Diagram 8-16 shows the alignment for the 2-2-1 Press Drill. The basketball is dribbled by player #1 into a double team at the ten-second line. G_1 and F_3 work on their timing for the trap and their right-angle positioning when the trap is made. All the players shift as the basketball moves. Once the trap is made, player #1 will pass to either #4, #3, or #5. For purposes of the

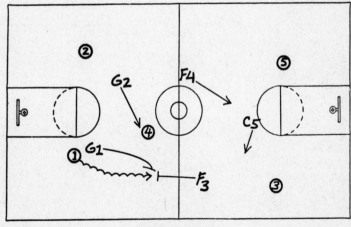

Diagram 8-16

drill, you should tell #1 what pass to make before he begins his dribble. This allows us to develop the proper coverage on defense. You can create different practice coverage situations in order to improve the defensive shifts. Many defensive weaknesses can be eliminated in this drill.

You may also designate the pass from #1 to #2 to #5. You can create any passing combination that you want, in order to practice defensive coverage. Diagrams 8-17, 8-18, and 8-19 illustrate certain combinations.

The defensive players may also be rotated at different positions. This helps promote each player's total understanding of the 2-2-1 full-court zone press.

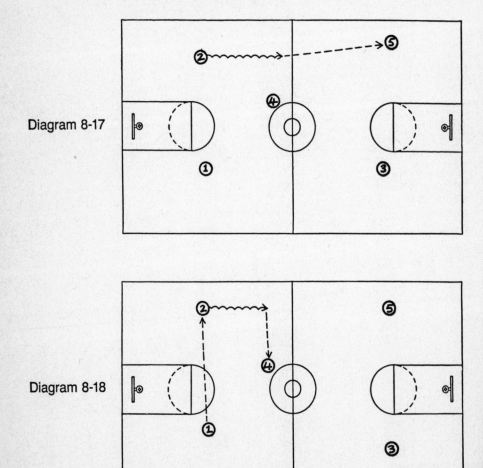

Diagram 8-17

Diagram 8-18

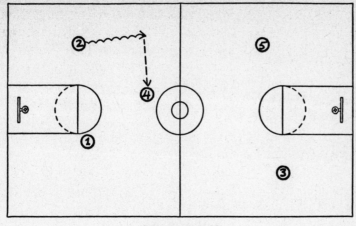

Diagram 8-19

9

Overplay-Pressure Man-Man Full-Court Defense and the 1-2-2 Zone Press

The third full-court defense of the Confusion System is the 1-2-2 zone press. This is a very aggressive type press with the defense executing the double-team situation as soon as possible. It is a defense that complements the man-man and 2-2-1 presses extremely well.

SIGNAL SYSTEM FOR CALLING DEFENSES

Hand Signals

For the man-man press we had the floater signaling with both hands below his waist immediately after a score. If we were to switch from the man-man press to the 2-2-1 press, the signal would be made by the floater raising both hands above his head. The call for the 1-2-2 zone press could easily be made by having the floater hold only one hand above his head. The floater must remember that the signal must be given immediately after his team scores.

Number Signal

A possible number system could also be devised to signal the type of defense. The call, "100" could signify full-court man-man pressure; "220" could signify the 2-2-1 zone press; "120" could signify the 1-2-2 zone press. Either the floater or the team captain could be responsible for making the defensive call.

Whatever system is used, the most important thing is for the team to be organized in their selections. Eighty percent of the time, the floater should have the defense aligned in the man-man press. If a team plays the full-court zone presses more than 20 percent of the time, their basic man-man defense at the full-court level may become sloppy and ineffective. The best defense is good one-on-one pressure, mixing the zone press to confuse things.

MAN-MAN ROTATION TO THE 1-2-2 PRESS

Front Three

Diagram 9-1 shows the defensive team moving from the man-man press while the basketball is out-of-bounds, to the 1-2-2 press as the ball is inbounded. G_2 cuts the receiver, #2, at the sideline. G_1 leaves the middle and goes to the basketball for the double team. F_3 moves from the weak side to the middle of the court to defend this area.

Because the initial trap went away from F_3, the front three men involved in the double team will be G_1, G_2, and F_3. If the ball has been inbounded and double-teamed on F_3's side, then the front three would have been G_1, G_2, and F_4. (Diagram 9-2.)

The point man on the press would be G_1. The wings then would be G_2, F_3, or F_4, depending on where the ball is inbounded and double-teamed.

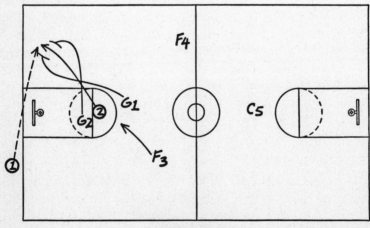

Diagram 9-1

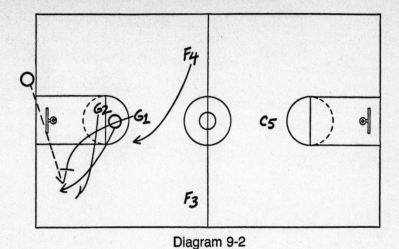

Diagram 9-2

Point Changes

Diagram 9-3 shows the inevitable happening. G_2 gets caught on the inside looking for the interception. A change of assignment must take place. G_1 quickly moves in for the double team, assuming the sideline position. G_2 now becomes the point man on the 1-2-2 press with G_1 assuming the wing position. When the basketball is passed to the opposite guard, #2 to #1, the front three make the proper shifts. This is shown in Diagram 9-4.

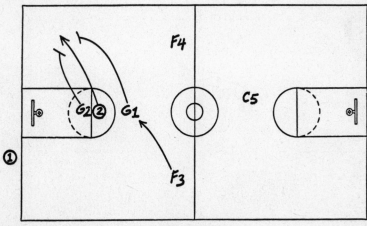

Diagram 9-3

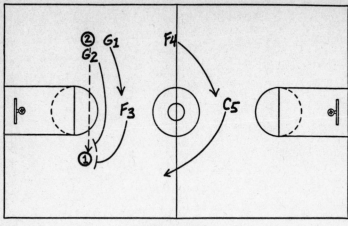

Diagram 9-4

Back Two

In Diagram 9-5 the inbounds reception of the pass has determined the designation of the front three. The location of the reception also determines the back two defenders. F_4 has responsibility for the strongside pass to #4, and C_5 has the deep pass responsibility.

In Diagram 9-6 the pass is returned from #2 to #1. The front three make their defensive shift. The back two exchange positions. F_4 has responsibility for the deep pass, and C_5 has responsibility for the strongside sideline pass.

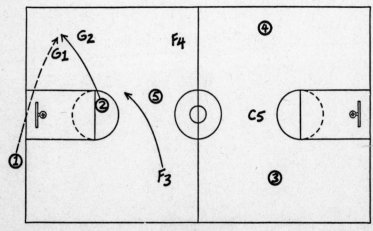

Diagram 9-5

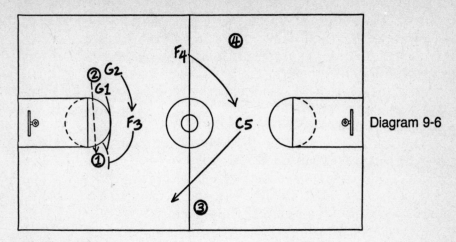

Diagram 9-6

Sideline Pass

In Diagram 9-7 player #1 passes to #3. C_5 makes certain that #3 can't penetrate via the dribble down the sideline. F_3 follows the pass and double teams #3 with C_5. F_4 favors the strong side and still has responsibility for the long pass to the basket. G_2 drops back deeply to help protect the deep middle and the basket. G_1 moves in to defend the shallow middle.

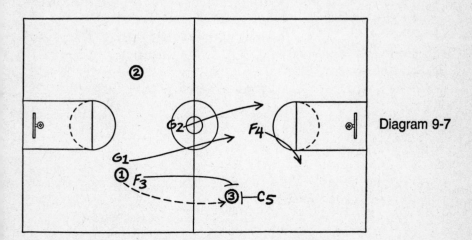

Diagram 9-7

1-2-2 PRESS TO THE HALF-COURT MAN-MAN OVERPLAY-PRESSURE DEFENSE

It is more difficult to get back into the man-man from the 1-2-2 press than from the 2-2-1 press. Because of the early traps in the 1-2-2 press, it is difficult to get the half-court man-man defense set up. It is difficult to beat the offense down the court if the defensive team is not totally alert.

The defense must give up the traps after the basketball crosses the ten-second line. The back two must jam the lane and not allow any penetration. The front three really hustle to get back and help defend the basket. It is vital that one of the defenders nearest the basketball take responsibility for halting the ball handler's advance. The dribbler must not be allowed downcourt unchallenged. This would result in penetration and a high percentage shot. Once the defense is inside the offense, we come away from the basket to the man-man.

The 1-2-2 zone press is an excellent complement to the man-man and 2-2-1 presses. It helps confuse the offense by exploiting the double-team situation that is created by the inbounds pass. Several quick scores can result with this press, and the defense dictates the tempo of the game.

PERSONNEL CHARACTERISTICS

Guards

Both guards should be intelligent and understand the press in its entirety. They must be able to read the double-team situation quickly. G_1 and G_2 must know instinctively by their positioning who will take the point and wing. They need to be tenacious, hard-working individuals who never quit.

Forwards and Center

The forwards have responsibility that is sometimes confusing to them. If the ball comes in play on F_4's side, F_3 is a wing trapper with G_1 and G_2. If the basketball comes in play on F_3's side, their roles are reversed.

Therefore, the forwards must be quite intelligent and possess the ability to make quick decisions. Indecisive players will not be able to function in this defensive system. The forwards should be able to anticipate the movement of the basketball in order to make the defense go. If they possess a long reach and the ability to anticipate, several interceptions will be created by their play.

C_5 has to be intelligent in reacting quickly to the first trap of the defense. He immediately has responsibility for all deep downcourt passes. This includes the deep crosscourt passes, like the pass from #2 to #3 in Diagram 9-8.

C_5 should possess the ability to move on the court quickly. It is critical for both forwards and the center to possess good speed. C_5 must understand or possess the ability to position himself at the proper angles of the court in order to create deflections and interceptions. This ability, to a great degree, is instinctive.

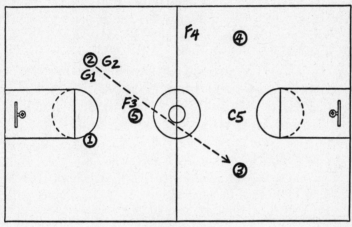

Diagram 9-8

Personnel Philosophy

We feel very strongly that a successful team must be able to play aggressively as well as intelligently from baseline to baseline. To promote this ability, we encourage our underclass teams to play overplay man-man exclusively. As players are developed in a program based on the man-to-man pressure defense, the improvement of these players is more dramatic in all skill areas as opposed to those underclass teams who use zone defenses. The boys who learn to play basketball in the man-man pressure defense will be aggressive, hustling players. Intensity is something that each player will learn by playing the man-man. It cannot be accomplished in one year; it is a part of a correlated program. Those players who are not willing to play hard will retire from the program.

Start your players hustling at an early age. By the time they are seniors, they won't turn to the bench looking for help from the coach in a tight game. They'll go out and attack their opponents and do something about the outcome of the game themselves. "He who hesitates is lost," is a valid statement.

INDIVIDUAL ASSIGNMENTS

Probably the most critical assignment for our players is to execute advantageous double-team situations. For example, if the inbounds guard receives the pass on the baseline, we need a tight, super-aggressive double team. The receiver is boxed in by our defenders and the baseline. If the defenders keep right angles to one another and fight the pass with their hands, the chance for an interception is extremely good. The potential for a weak lob pass is highly favorable. Diagram 9-9 shows this situation.

The men involved in the double team should also learn to read the situations. If the offensive player is in a position where he has a lot of floor to work with, the trap may be less intense. It is definitely to the advantage of the defense to vary the tightness of the double team to help confuse the ball handler. It will help keep the offense from establishing a smooth tempo in attacking the defense. If the tempo has shifted entirely to the defense, then the double-team personnel should go after the ball handler aggressively. Diagram 9-10 shows a loose double-team situation.

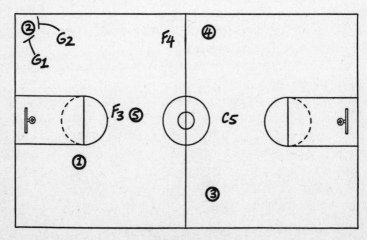

Diagram 9-9

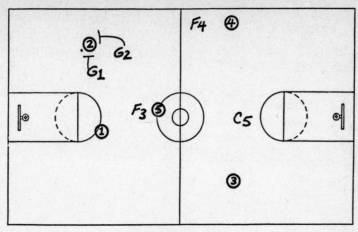

Diagram 9-10

Another important personnel assignment is that of positioning. The defenders utilizing the double-team method must learn
individual positioning in order to promote the best floor angle
for the interception. This concept goes back to our half-court
man-man defense. The players must learn how to position
themselves on the court in relation to their men and the
basketball. The defender must always have a mental edge on the
offensive man. By positioning correctly the defender is controlling what the offensive man can and cannot do. It is your
responsibility to watch the passing carefully and then help the
defenders with their floor angle positioning in order to improve
their chances of creating a turnover. Positioning is taught in all
our defensive drills, and this should help when you explain
positioning in full-court situations.

Another important floor positioning occurs during the
double team. The defenders involved in the double team must
know the limits of distance that they can play in relation to the
ball handler. Forcing a change in the arch of the pass goes along
with the knowledge of this relationship. Quick, sharp passes
must never be allowed. The defense could never shift quickly
enough to keep up with this type of passing.

SPECIAL DEFENSIVE SIGNALS

Diagram 9-11 shows a trapping situation that is not predeter-
mined by a hand or verbal signal. This trap is keyed by who
receives the inbounds pass, and where it is received.

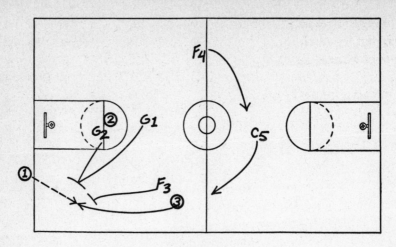

Diagram 9-11

The offensive forward, #3, makes his cut to the strongside baseline and receives the inbounds pass. G_2 moves in for the double team, and G_1 denies the pass to the middle in the 1-2-2 press.

This is an automatic trap and an automatic call for the 1-2-2 press. Even though a 2-2-1 press may have been the call, we go with the 1-2-2 because of the convenience of the situation. With the offensive forward getting the basketball on the baseline, a natural 1-2-2 zone press is created.

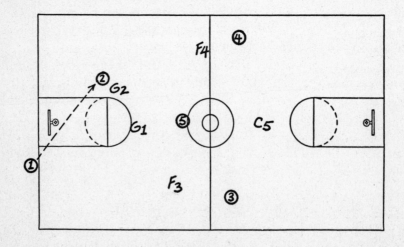

Diagram 9-12

Another special trapping situation may be called by the coach. For example, call "0-120" means that the defense does not switch from the out-of-bounds man-man press to the 1-2-2 zone press until after two passes have been completed. Diagram 9-12 shows this defensive maneuver.

Player #1 passes to #2. The defense remains in the man-man press with G_1 favoring the middle. Diagram 9-13 continues the sequence with #2 passing back to #1.

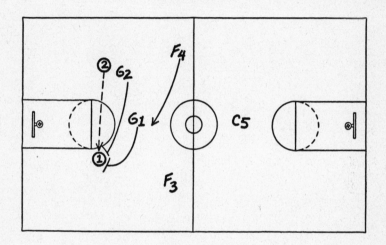

Diagram 9-13

When #1 receives the second pass from #2, G_1 picks his man up with double-team help from G_2. F_4 moves to the middle from the weak side to help defend this area. F_4 is also conscious of a possible interception of a third pass from #1 to #2. F_3 defends the strongside pass downcourt to #3 or #4.

SPECIAL MAN-MAN ROTATION AND THE 2-1-2 PRESS

Combining the man-man and the 2-1-2 press is sometimes highly disirable. This is especially effective against those teams that prefer to use a 2-1-2 offensive set when breaking full-court presses. Diagram 9-14 shows the defensive switch from the man-man to the 2-1-2 zone press.

Player #2 receives the inbounds pass from #1. G_2 takes #2 just as he would in the 2-2-1 zone press. G_1 stays to cover the middle. The weakside guard, #1. F_3 and G_2 are now the defensive guards and play their men as they would in the 2-2-1 except they may pressure more from the weak side to make it look more like a man-man.

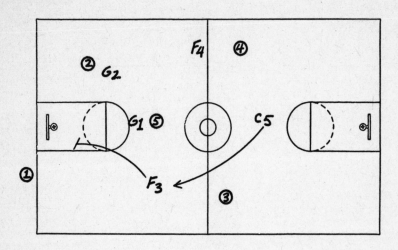

Diagram 9-14

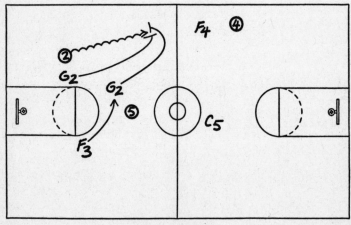

Diagram 9-15

Eventually, one of the dribbling guards would be pushed up the side of the floor toward the ten-second line. As the dribbler reaches the coffin corner, G_1 moves outside for the double team. The weakside guard, either F_3 or G_2, would replace G_1 in the middle as shown in Diagram 9-15.

The roles of F_3 and F_4 would be reversed if the inbounds pass comes in on F_3's side. In Diagram 9-15, C_5 and F_4 are basically playing #3 and #4 man -to-man as long as there is an offensive middle man in a 2-1-2 offensive set. If the offense goes to a 2-2-1 set as shown in Diagram 9-16, the assignments of C_5 and F_4 are the same as they would be in the 1-2-2 zone press.

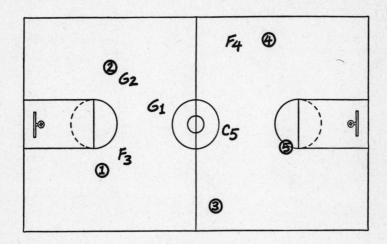

Diagram 9-16

Press Drill (1-2-2)

Diagram 9-17 shows the inbounds pass coming to #2. G_1 traps with G_2, F_3 moves to defend the middle, and F_4 plays the strongside sideline pass.

Diagram 9-18 shows the No Post Drill. Player #2 starts at the foul line with G_2 defending. G_1 assumes his position as the floater in the drill. Once #2 receives the pass, a weakside guard steps on the court for the offensive team as shown. The weakside forward moves up to cover the pass from #2 to #1. F_4 would not participate unless the inbounds pass had been completed on the opposite side. In that case, he would have assumed the same role as F_3.

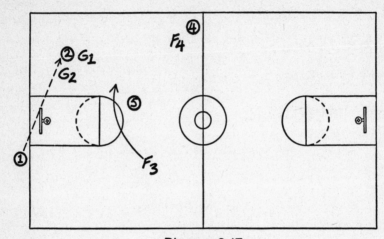

Diagram 9-17

Middle Post Drill

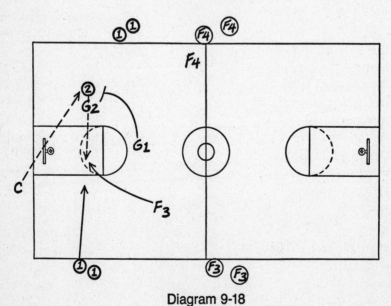

Diagram 9-18

No Post Drill

10

Body Building and Conditioning Programs for Defensive Strength and Quickness

A strong body is necessary for skillful defensive play. A physically weak player does not have the lateral quickness necessary to prevent the offensive player from gaining an advantage. This type of defender is always a step slower in his attempt to control the movement of his offensive opponent. He is also slow in his ability to stay ahead of the full-court transition game. Slow foot speed and overall poor endurance are other characteristics of the physically weak defender.

Being physically strong enables the defender to easily utilize his own skeletal frame. Through a proper weight and conditioning program, the defender should be able to improve his quickness, speed, agility, jumping ability, and stamina. Many players understand the fundamentals and possess the correct skills to be successful but never reach their potential because of a lack of physical strength. Once an opponent steps on the court, strength becomes a key ingredient in every player's ability to compete.

WEIGHT LIFTING IN AND OUT OF THE SEASON

In Season

Our weight program during the basketball season is not as extensive as during the off-season. Time is the biggest limitation. With all the time that must be devoted to developing basketball skills, it becomes very difficult to find a time block for weight training during the practice session. Most coaches spend practice sessions developing shooting techniques, individual offensive and defensive skills, offensive and defensive team skills, and conclude practice sessions with free throw shooting and wind sprints. There seems to be no feasible place for weight training during practice.

Weight training during the season can only be accomplished if you are willing to alter your practice routines. A solution to this problem, which works for us, is to substitute weight training for wind sprints at the conclusion of practice. We also borrow a few minutes from other practice situations until we set aside a 20-25 minute block of time at the end of practice for weight training.

What happens to the team when wind sprints are no longer run daily but only every other day? Nothing! You simply allow for an an ample amount of running during the general practice session to replace the lost time spent for weight training. Our players are active in drills and team situations during practice and receive ample conditioning. It is your responsibility to structure an aggressive practice situation and allow the drills to help condition the players.

The workout that concludes our practice session involves using our two weight machines and our isokinetic leg strength machine: "the jumper." The Isokinetics Sales Company officially labels their machine the R. V. Jumper. We work out every other day. Following is the recommended workout schedule for the jumper as published by the manufacturer:

Speed Set	Number of Repetitions	Number of Sets
No. 1	40	1
No. 2	35	1
No. 3	30	1
No. 4	20	1
No. 5	10	1

After a participant completes one set on the R. V. Jumper, he moves to a weight machine. Each athlete is asked to complete three weight exercises before he moves back to the R. V. Jumper for another set.

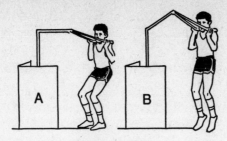

Diagram 10-1

Diagram 10-1 shows the athlete placing himself under the shoulder pads of the R. V. Jumper. He explodes from the "A" jumping position to the "B" position with his toes fully extended.

Also mounted on top of the machine is a speedometer. This helps show the amount of exertion needed by the participant to gain maximum benefit from the machine. Following is the manufacturer's speed chart:

Speed 1	30-40 MPH
Speed 2	26-36 MPH
Speed 3	22-32 MPH
Speed 4	18-24 MPH
Speed 5	10-20 MPH

We feel that the R. V. Jumper, if used properly, improves overall body strength, speed, quickness, agility, and adds inches to the player's jumping ability. Our conditioning program is built on the R. V. Jumper.

The three weight stations used are the Tri-Extension, Pulley Chins, and Military Press.

Tri-Extension Exercise

Number of Repetitions	Number of Sets	Weight
10	1	Maximum
8	1	Maximum
6	1	Maximum
4	1	Maximum
2	1	Maximum

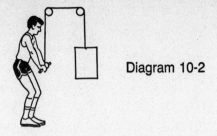

Diagram 10-2

Diagram 10-2 shows the athlete pulling the attached weight to a complete extension from his head to below his waist. We feel that this will help strengthen those muscles used in rebounding.

Pully Chin Exercise

Number of Repetitions	Number of Sets	Weight
10	1	Maximum
9	1	Maximum
6	1	Maximum
4	1	Maximum
2	1	Maximum

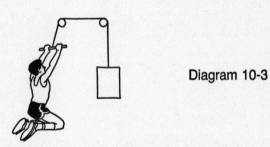

Diagram 10-3

Diagram 10-3 shows the athlete pulling the weight down from above his head to his chest. Again, we feel that this is another exercise that adds strength in bringing the basketball to the chest for possession.

Military Press Exercise

Number of Repetitions	Number of Sets	Weight
10	1	Maximum
8	1	Maximum
6	1	Maximum
4	1	Maximum
2	1	Maximum

Diagram 10-4

The military press is executed in the sitting position, as shown in Diagram 10-4. The athlete keeps his back erect and lifts the weight above his head. This helps strengthen the arms. Basketball is a game where the hands are held above the shoulders much of the time. This exercise helps strengthen the shoulder muscles that hold the arms above the head.

Out of Season

The out of season workout is a little more extensive. Our program is based on the R. V. Jumper. Over a twelve-week program, we can improve a player's jumping ability by several inches. Following is the twelve-week program:

Week One

Speed Set	Number of Repetitions	Number of Sets
No. 1	40	1
No. 2	35	1
No. 3	30	1
No. 4	20	1
No. 5	10	1

Week Two

No. 1	42	1
No. 2	37	1
No. 3	32	1
No. 4	22	1
No. 4	12	1

Week Three

No. 1	44	1
No. 2	39	1
No. 3	34	1

| No. 4 | 24 | 1 |
| No. 5 | 14 | 1 |

Week Four

No. 1	46	1
No. 2	41	1
No. 3	36	1
No. 4	26	1
No. 5	16	1

Week Five

No. 1	48	1
No. 2	43	1
No. 3	38	1
No. 4	28	1
No. 5	18	1

Week Six

No. 1	50	1
No. 2	45	1
No. 3	40	1
No. 4	30	1
No. 5	20	1

Week Seven

No. 1	52	1
No. 2	47	1
No. 3	42	1
No. 4	32	1
No. 5	22	1

Week Eight

No. 1	54	1
No. 2	49	1
No. 3	44	1
No. 4	34	1
No. 5	24	1

Week Nine

No. 1	56	1
No. 2	51	1
No. 3	46	1
No. 4	36	1
No. 5	26	1

Week Ten

No. 1	58	1
No. 2	53	1
No. 3	48	1
No. 4	38	1
No. 5	28	1

Week Eleven

No. 1	60	1
No. 2	55	1
No. 3	50	1
No. 4	40	1
No. 5	30	1

To continue the program to the twelfth week or beyond, the repetitions for the eleventh week are followed.

WEIGHT TRAINING

Bench Press

Exercises that we add to our training program out of season are varied. We have our players bench press to help build upper body strength as shown in Diagram 10-5. We use the same amount of repetitions.

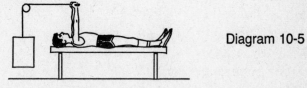

Diagram 10-5

Number of Repetitions	Number of Sets	Weight
10	1	Maximum
8	1	Maximum
6	1	Maximum
4	1	Maximum
2	1	Maximum

Wrist And Forearm Extensions

We also use this exercise to help strengthen those muscles used when gripping the basketball. With the pronated and supinated grips we roll a heavy weight up a rope by repeatedly turning the handle as shown in Diagram 10-6.

Diagram 10-6

Number of Repetitions	Number of Sets	Weight
10	1	Maximum
8	1	Maximum
6	1	Maximum
4	1	Maximum
2	1	Maximum

Additions

We add another series to the Bench Press and Pulley Chins. To revise these exercises the athlete moves the lifting and pulling positions to the back of the shoulders.

ISOMETRICS AND PEAKING YOUR TEAM

We always make a total effort to peak our team for the state tournament near the conclusion of the season. Not only do we want our players at the top of their physical conditioning but also at the top of their mental conditioning. We want the players to *believe* that they have an edge in physical conditioning going into tournament play. This may be done by either altering or adding to our conditioning program during the final weeks of the season. We enjoy adding a few simple isometric exercises to our daily practice schedule.

We use an isometric rope which can be a clothesline nine feet in length, slid through two rubber grips for the hands. A garden hose could be cut for the grips.

Pull-Up Exercise

For upper body strength we use the Pull-Up Exercise. The athlete stands on the rope with the feet shoulder-width apart. He then uses the hands in a pronated position and pulls upward for ten seconds.

Ankles-In Exercise

In the Ankles-In Exercise the athlete sits on the floor with his legs extended. For ten seconds he pressures each ankle against the other.

Ankles-Crossed Exercise

Again, the athlete is setting on the floor. For ten seconds he attempts to pull his feet through one another.

Leg Push-Out Exercise

In the Leg Push-Out Exercise we have the athlete lay on his back with his knees pulled to his chest. Two strands of the rope are placed over the shoe sole and a handle is grasped on each side of the thighs. For ten seconds he pushes out with his legs and feet.

RUNNING PROGRAM FOR IN AND OUT OF SEASON

Many coaches believe in long distance running to help condition the heart and lungs. They feel that this promotes endurance. We do not disagree with this philosophy, but we simply don't have the time for this type of conditioning. We concentrate on sprints instead. We try to exercise the athlete in drills that simulate the type of running that will be done in a game. Here are some of the conditioning drills that we use.

Forward and Backward Sprints

The athlete starts at the baseline and sprints to the opposite end of the court. When he reaches the far baseline, he backpedals to his original position.

Forward-Backpedal Sprints

The athlete starts at he baseline and begins to sprint to the opposite end of the court. On the whistle, he reverses direction and begins to backpedal. On the next whistle he resumes sprinting forward.

Reverse Direction Sprint

The athlete starts at the baseline and sprints downcourt. When the whistle blows, the athlete reverses direction and sprints back toward the starting point. Each time the coach blows the whistle the athlete reverses the direction of his sprint.

Reverse Direction Sprint-Shuffle

The drill is the same as the Reverse Direction Sprint Drill with one exception. If the coach blows the whistle twice, the athlete reverses direction, assumes his defensive stance and shuffles forward.

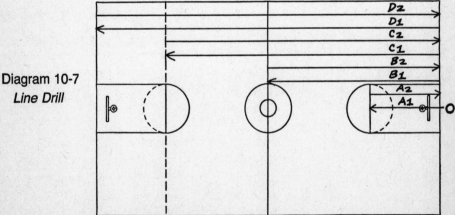

Diagram 10-7
Line Drill

Line Drill

Diagram 10-7 shows the Line Drill being executed. The athlete starts at the baseline. He sprints to the foul line and back, to the ten-second line and back, to the far foul line and back, and finally to the far baseline and back. To force the athlete to extend himself, the coach may wish to put a time limitation on this drill.

Index